Table of Contents

v — ABOUT THE AUTHOR

viii — FOREWORD

xi — INTRODUCTION

1 — CHAPTER 1
Nature-Based Learning and Early Childhood Education

21

55 — CHAPTER 3
Nature-Based Learning and Play

91 — CHAPTER 4
Growing Strong Nature-Based Educators

109 — CHAPTER 5
Visioning and Managing a Nature-Based Program

139 — INDEX

About the Author

Monica Wiedel-Lubinski has pursued her love of nature-based education for nearly three decades. She began her career at Irvine Nature Center in Owings Mills, Maryland where she founded Maryland's second licensed, NAEYC-accredited nature preschool. She directed a broad range of nature-based programs for children, families, and teachers spanning her 19-year tenure there. After her resignation, she received the Margaret O'Neil Award in 2017 in recognition of her outstanding accomplishments in nature-based education.

Recognizing the need for nature-based teacher training and professional networks, Monica Wiedel-Lubinski founded the Association for Nature-Based Education (ANBE) in 2016 with support from colleagues across the region. This led to the creation of the Nature-Based Teacher Certification, a 36-hour course which over 2,000 teachers have completed, hailing from all 50 states and 25 different countries. She has founded/co-founded three nature-based preschool programs in the greater Baltimore, MD area including the forest preschool at Carrie Murray Nature Center in Baltimore and Notchcliff Nature Programs in Glen Arm, MD. She consults to help countless others breathe life into new nature-based programs and schools.

As co-chair of the Outdoor Preschool Licensing Advisory Team, Monica spearheads a group of stakeholders in Maryland advocating for more equitable, inclusive access to nature-based learning. The team successfully passed House Bill 525 in 2023 to launch an outdoor preschool pilot in Maryland, second in the U.S. to do so.

She earned a bachelor's degree in K-12 Art Education and a master's degree in early childhood education at Towson University, Baltimore, MD. In 2024, Monica completed a year-long fellowship at UMBC in the Maryland Early Childhood Leadership Program (MECLP), in partnership with the Shriver Center at the University of Massachusetts in Boston.

Most of all, Monica loves to slow down and unplug, sharing wild adventures with her husband and two children in the forest, streams, and meadows of Maryland where they reside.

Dedication

To my husband and partner in life, Nick, whose constant support has allowed me to blossom in this work; to my children who endlessly inspire me; and to my parents who gifted me with a love of nature.

Acknowledgements

This book is a result of many open hearts, curious minds, and wise souls starting with the children, families, and teachers I have come to know over years in this field. I want to express my gratitude to those who have helped breathe life into this book, because this is not a journey I take alone. To Irvine Nature Center, thank you for being the kind of organization that allowed me to ask questions alongside children and grow through shared nature connection. The lessons I learned at Irvine will forever be part of my heart and essential to my work in nature-based education. To my colleagues and the families who shared photos, stories, and helpful edits of this book, you illustrate nature-based education at its best, and I am grateful for your contributions. To Emily Woodmansee, thank you for reviewing the book with a critical eye and offering endless support over the years. To the members, staff, and Board of the Association for Nature-Based Education, thank you for your steady encouragement to make contributions to our field to help build capacity for our important work. To David Sobel, your writing and research has inspired me for decades and it is an honor to include your foreword here. I am especially grateful to Dana Battaglia, my editor at NAEYC, for her perseverance on this book, shepherding the process for over five years to bring it to the world of early childhood education. Finally, to my husband and children who understand my passion for nature-based education and offered constant support to help me bring this book to life.

Foreword

How lucky you are to have picked up this book. If you're looking to bring nature-based education to your preschool or elementary school curriculum, you've come to the right place. If you're a parent wondering about whether to put your child in a nature preschool program, this book will convince you that's a "right as rain decision" decision.

Monica, the author, is the real deal. She's been on the nature-based early childhood path for more than a couple of decades. She taught at and founded the Irvine Nature Preschool in Maryland and then went on to start a couple of other urban nature preschools. She's advised dozens of other preschools, she's taught hundreds of teacher professional development workshops and courses and she recently played a major role in getting legislation passed for an outdoor preschool licensing program in Maryland. It's just the second such program in the country and it wouldn't have happened without Monica's deep experience and guidance. She can get dirty making mudpies with children and then get dressed up to converse in the halls of government.

Monica has taken all the raw material of what she has learned and experienced over the last 25 years and boiled it down into this book—like taking 40 gallons of maple sap and transforming it into one gallon of glistening, sweet maple syrup. But she doesn't sugarcoat the seriousness of nature education outdoors with children. She identifies the joys, and the challenges, and provides sage advice of how to move your program, step-by-step, more fully outside.

This book is a soup-to-nuts guide. Looking for a recipe for dandelion fritters? It's in here. Looking for how to talk to anxious parents? She's got your back. Got a problem with how to handle all that stick play? She'll help you figure out how to develop a risk management plan. But before getting into more reasons for why you'll find this book valuable, let's consider one of the big reasons why Monica, and many of us across the country, want to nudge early childhood education outdoors. Let me tell you a story.

My wife and I recently put up an adhered to the glass bird feeders. It quickly became a source of constant joy—titmice, goldfinches, chickadees, and wrens so close we could almost touch them. But, of course, the wily squirrels discovered the feeder and tried every trick in the book to figure out how to access the seed. My wife's response was to jump up, pound on the window, or run out onto the porch yelling, *"Bad squirrel! Bad squirrel! Get out of here! Shoo!"* It's a never-ending battle.

One day, our four-year-old granddaughter, Greta, was here for the day when the squirrel assault began. My wife, her grandmother known as Nana, went on the offensive with the "bad squirrel" invective. She came back inside as the squirrel ran off, and Greta said to her, *"Nana, maybe it's a good squirrel."* Ah hah! This, I thought, is why we want to connect children and nature. There is an implicit, biophilic, sense of the goodness of animals and plants in children. It's born into us and if we want children to grow up to love nature and be environmentally responsible adults, we need to capitalize on the critical period of affinity for nature in early childhood.

That's the big idea underlying this book. Affirming the goodness of connecting children to nature has a raft of benefits. Let me articulate the many ways Monica helps us understand those benefits and then figure out how to make programs move outside and thrive.

First, Monica puts the nature-based early childhood movement in the context of other educational movements and the history of environmental education. She provides a dash of evolutionary theory, touching on our biological heritage as hunter-gatherers, and articulates why children being in nature is, well, natural. She weaves in an understanding of indigenous ways of knowing and how we can learn from our Native American forbears. And she articulates the importance of making this approach accessible to families of all means, not just white kids in the suburbs.

Next, she summarizes and makes accessible a vast array of research on how nature-based play and learning is healthy for child development. Parents often like the looks of nature preschool, but they've got lots of questions. Will my child be ready for elementary school? Will they learn their letters and numbers? Is it healthy for my child to be out in the cold and rain? What about learning to follow rules and directions? Monica summarizes the research on language learning, resilience and executive function development, social and emotional skills, imagination and creativity, and more. She provides a one-stop research shop for how to answer all the questions from parents and skeptical administrations.

After that she gets into the nitty-gritty of how to organize your day, how to document children's learning and growth, what parents need to know about outfitting their children for being outside in all seasons, how to support differently-abled children, how to set up the schedule for the day. (I particularly like her articulation of the 50/50 principle.) She really leaves no stone unturned. And she also makes it clear why letting children turn over stones is important.

All of this wisdom is laced through with illustrative photos, clarifying graphics, and guidelines for dealing with problem behaviors. She's engaged emergent leaders from around the country to describe their innovative rural and urban programs. Attiya Wells' Backyard Basecamp in Baltimore, Maryfaith Decker Miller's Forest Learning Collaborative in upstate New York, and Ashley Brailsford's Unearthing Joy programs in Nashville are just some of the chorus of diverse voices she presents.

Really, this is a handy book. Nature-based early childhood education has finally come of age and Monica is a big part of why that has happened. I hope you appreciate the wisdom she has to share.

—**David Sobel, M.Ed.**
Professor Emeritus
Education Department
Antioch University New England
Keene, New Hampshire

Introduction

Learning in nature is certainly not a new concept. It is as old as time and human existence. But in recent years, a renewed interest to unplug and get back to basics has brought this movement to the forefront of early childhood education. Until now, nature-based approaches have been loosely lumped into a bucket containing environmental education, outdoor education, or recreation, unless a school or program explicitly refers to itself as a forest or nature preschool, forest kindergarten, or something similarly named. As it stands, nature-based early childhood education (NBECE) consists of predominantly middle- and upper-income families and is difficult for most low-resourced families to access.

This book provides a definition of NBECE as it is applied in American early childhood settings. Furthermore, NBECE is defined as its own educational philosophy. This definition is based on my perspective as an educator, founding director of three nature-based preschool programs, advocate for local and national initiatives in early childhood environmental education, and proponent of playful nature-based learning. My experience has unfolded over more than two decades, rooted in the greater Baltimore-Washington, DC, metropolitan region and now reaching practitioners across the United States and around the globe. On a more personal note, my roles as aunt and mother are also inseparable from the beliefs and practices that follow in this book. This is all to say that there are many facets of nature-based education and many ways to serve and support one another. This longing to provide access, build capacity, and nurture deep nature connection is what frames my vision. I share my story here to help color the experiences that have led me to writing this book.

Blazing A Trail in Nature-Based Education

For more than two decades I have pondered, tested, and revised my views on nature pedagogy and nature-based education. As the founding director of a licensed, NAEYC-accredited nature preschool at Irvine Nature Center in Owings Mills, Maryland, I began to find my way. From my earliest moments leading a Children's Nature Series in 1998 until it grew into a full-fledged preschool in 2009, I had countless days of joy in the field but also felt great failure and frustration. I have always shared the children's sincere sense of wonder and curiosity about the natural world, but translating outdoor learning into a preschool program is not nearly as straightforward as that.

As the director of a nature preschool, I was confronted with typical tasks: creating policies, aligning curriculum with standards, performing assessments, overseeing enrollment, collecting tuition, connecting with parents, training the staff … you get the picture. The *real* challenge was to find a way to accomplish these tasks while underscoring the power of nature-based learning. In other words, remaining true to our vision. At the time, there was seemingly no guidance for nature preschool directors like me. I was aware of the Dodge Nature Center in West St. Paul, Minnesota, and Audubon Naturalist Society's Nature Preschool in Chevy Chase, Maryland. Beyond that, I knew of only about a dozen or so programs in the United States that were nature preschools. There was a lot I needed to learn. I came to realize that we needed to build a network to find support.

My time at the nature center proved invaluable. I became a naturalist by lived experience on the trails, by finding answers to questions alongside curious little children. I was forced to dig deep and learn how to be more flexible, more patient, and more forgiving. I developed programs for diverse audiences of children and teachers in low-resourced communities in Baltimore, which was in stark contrast to the population attending the nature preschool. I collaborated on a remarkable nature play-space project, harnessing the ideas and skills of volunteers, teachers, and children. Significantly, I also began to lead professional development courses for other teachers.

As I inched further along on my journey, more and more teachers would seek out advice from our growing nature preschool. This longing for relevant training and networking crystallized my desire to grow the movement of NBECE and to help other teachers succeed.

After resigning from Irvine Nature Center in 2016, more determined than ever to form a nonprofit association to support nature-based educators, I got to work. And with tremendous encouragement from regional founding members, we launched the nonprofit Eastern Region Association of Forest and Nature Schools to provide services, support, and inspiration to early childhood professionals to advance the field of NBECE and encourage lifelong appreciation for our natural world. In 2024, we officially became the Association for Nature-Based Education (ANBE) to better reflect our national reach and to more aptly describe our mission's work.

Even as ANBE was beginning to take root, I had the honor of co-founding a forest preschool program at Carrie Murray Nature Center in Baltimore, starting in 2017. This beautiful vision for more equitable access to NBECE in Baltimore coalesced alongside two visionary colleagues, Monica French and Mepi Neill, under the guidance of Mary Hardcastle at Baltimore City Recreation and Parks. As a third offering to my local community, ANBE launched Notchcliff Nature Programs with an immersive forest preschool at Glen Meadows Retirement Community in Glen Arm, Maryland, in 2018.

My journey, paired with the significant contributions of my fellow colleagues, has led me to identify the following "7 Principles of Nature-Based Early Childhood Education." In the spirit of helping other educators like you, I hope these principles will provide solid footing for your professional journey. Ponder them. Challenge them. And blaze your own understanding.

7 Principles of Nature-Based Early Childhood Education

1. **Nature** is the central organizing feature of the curriculum, school, or program for children ages birth to 8 years old. Children learn in, about, with, and as a part of the natural world (Bailie 2012; Bailie & Finch 2015; NAAEE 2019; Sobel 2016).

2. **Direct experiences** with nature, natural materials, and outdoor environments take place in every season, in all kinds of weather (NAAEE 2019).

3. **Learning is child-directed** and occurs during playful, emergent outdoor experiences (NAAEE 2019). Inquiry, observation, and creative problem solving emerge as children discover seasonal surprises. The underlying processes behind learning are valued above end products.

4. **Children freely make choices and take risks.** Children are respected as capable learners who are afforded time, space, and permission to make independent decisions. Children are empowered and supported in appropriate risk-taking (NAAEE 2019).

5. **Teachers are facilitators** who guide meaningful learning opportunities and manage risks. Teachers have knowledge of developmentally appropriate practices in early childhood education and environmental education (NAAEE 2019; Sobel 2016). Teachers ensure safety and provide individualized accommodations to support every child's needs.

6. **Place-based underpinnings** honor the land, local ecosystem, Indigenous culture, and the diversity found in both natural and human communities. The quest for environmental justice, equity, diversity, and inclusion is inseparable from cultivating respect for all living things.

7. **Values promote environmental literacy and ecological identity** through a shared vision of personal responsibility to care for each other and the natural world (Brusaferro 2020; NAAEE 2019; Sobel 2016). Values of empathy, gratitude, kindness, respect, caretaking, and perseverance are reflected in the sustainable practices and ethos of the learning community.

NBECE is already being applied in a growing number of forest and nature preschools and is spreading into every imaginable early learning environment. As you examine the many facets of nature-based education presented, I hope you will discover why it has become an essential approach in modern-day early childhood education.

Using This Book

Each chapter contains topics that form the backbone of a nature pedagogy framework. The concepts and practices presented here are enmeshed in a holistic, nature-based approach to teaching and learning. This makes it challenging to address certain topics in only one chapter because they interrelate and overlap. As you read, keep in mind that each part is interconnected to the whole. Each chapter explores specific topics and strategies, but none of these components stand alone in practice.

At the opening of each chapter, you will find Guiding Questions as a starting point for reading. There are further Reflection Questions at the conclusion of each chapter to encourage more thought about what you have read. These questions may challenge previously held beliefs or practices as you examine how to apply new knowledge to your unique setting. The teacher's Call to Action in each chapter is a related challenge to help you deepen your understanding of nature pedagogy.

Each chapter also includes examples of how NBECE is applied in programs across the United States, along with beautiful photos from nature-based programs. Research and best practices from nature-based early childhood education experts provide diverse perspectives for you to consider. **(References for this book can be found at https://www.naeyc.org/resources/pubs/nature-based-ece)** Vignettes in each chapter offer insight from nature-based educators and administrators embedded in the field and illustrate the power of NBECE with young children. Templates are shared to help you implement the strategies provided. There are many more facets to examine in this rapidly expanding field, and while this book covers a lot of ground, there are still stones left unturned. Let this book be a resource to you, one that you can scribble notes in the margin, discuss with families at pickup, or share with colleagues over lunch as you strive to improve outcomes for your precious students. Use it as a springboard to hone your craft as an educator. You may move between chapters or features of interest, skip to the resources in the appendix, or read it cover to cover. However you choose to connect with this book, I sincerely hope you find seeds of inspiration that benefit children and our natural world.

CHAPTER 1

Nature-Based Learning and Early Childhood Education

Perhaps the most obvious reason that families enroll children in nature-based programs is that they want their children to develop a love of nature. Often referred to as "nature connection," this is a fundamental way of deepening our relationship with the marvelous home we know as Earth. This may sound like a lofty goal, but with time in nature beginning at birth, nature connection is a relationship that grows over a lifetime. It comes from observation and interaction outside, usually in the local landscape. When children have time, space, and permission to be outdoors and explore the natural world, a deeper understanding of nature's intricacies comes into focus. Direct, hands-on experiences provide sensory input that heightens awareness about the many facets of nature. Children develop meaningful personal relationships, not separate from, but rather, integral to our natural community. In turn, this evolving nature connection shapes ecological identity. As we consider how children's ecological identities emerge and change over time, this chapter offers helpful references about human relationships with nature (Brusaferro 2020; Kellert & Wilson 1993).

There are many dimensions to nature pedagogy that go beyond idealized visions of children laughing and frolicking in the sunshine. This chapter examines complex factors and concepts that form the bedrock of nature-based early childhood education. Key historical references shed light on how nature-based education came to be, calling attention to prominent figures and movements for greater context. This chapter touches on the kindred spirits of early childhood education by noting other educational models that share a love of nature in their practices. Not least of all, we touch on critical discussion about topics of environmental justice, diversity, equity, and inclusion to frame access to nature-based early childhood education (NBECE) as a basic right for all children.

Children make a fairy village at Bluestone Village and Nature Programs in Shohola, Pennsylvania.

CREDIT: BLUESTONE VILLAGE AND NATURE PROGRAMS.

Guiding Questions

As you read through this chapter, consider the following questions:

- What mainstream pedagogy might be similar to NBECE?

- What may have sparked the rise in NBECE?

- Who makes up the audience of NBECE?

- Why is environmental justice part of the discussion about NBECE?

- Why do you feel compelled to learn more about NBECE?

The Human-Nature Connection

The connection between humans and nature has its roots in how humans lived and developed as a species. There are hidden biological and evolutionary factors at work when it comes to our affinity for nature (Boyd et al. 2011; Seymour 2016; and Yang et al. 2023). Scientists have and continue to explore the interplay of genetic, ecological, social, and cultural aspects of our nature connection to better understand how people are predisposed to relate to the natural world and other living things. Given the history of our species on Earth, 99 percent of our time in existence has been in hunter-gatherer societies where we lived intimately with and depended completely on knowledge about the natural world for survival (Wilson 1984). There is an undeniable connection between people and nature.

NOTE: *The term* nature *is used broadly to describe green spaces with natural or open areas, usually containing trees, plants, and animals. Examples of green spaces may include habitats such as a park, garden, forest, meadow, stream, seashore, or desert.*

Our connection to nature plays a key role in how we develop both physically and mentally. The interest in the human-nature connection has increased in recent years as the links to nature's human-health benefits, including stress reduction, have been found. Nurturing this connection in young children is the foundation for NBECE.

The Beginnings of Nature Study

Before the concept of nature-based early childhood education was born, many political, environmental, and societal factors were at work. By the end of the nineteenth century, many scientists and scholars agreed that nature study was an ideal mode of nature-based learning and science inquiry in elementary schools (Kohlstedt 2005). One such book that supported nature study was Wilbur Jackman's *Nature Study for the Common School*, published in 1891. There was great enthusiasm behind the nature study movement, which gave rise to the creation of the American Nature Study Society (ANSS) in 1908. Established by progressive educators and scientists, ANSS proponents knew that nature connection was about more than scientific concepts. Nature study offered outdoor learning in schools with an aim to help children grow to love nature (Bailey 1904). Anna Botsford Comstock, the first female professor at Cornell University, penned *The Handbook for Nature Study*, which is still widely referenced today by nature-based educators (Comstock 1918).

In terms of public health, tuberculosis was a leading cause of death in the early twentieth century, which led to an international movement to create "open air" schools for children suffering with the illness (Pruitt 2020). These open-air schools allowed children to breathe fresh air by meeting in converted buildings with large windows or doors, on rooftops of schools, under pavilions, or in three-sided, shed-like structures. Children received hot meals, intentional rest times, and access to on-site physicians and dieticians for care. Proponents believed that exposure to sunshine and fresh air would help children heal and thrive with these interventions (known as heliotherapy) when compared with home or hospital settings. The movement began in Germany in 1904 when pediatrician Hermann Neufert opened a *Waldschule für kränkliche Kinder* ("forest school for sickly children"). The concept soon spread to the United States with the first open-air (or "fresh air") school opening in Providence, Rhode Island, in 1908 (Pruitt 2020; Quinn 1946). The children saw enormous health benefits attending these schools, including weight gain and a reduction in the spread of tuberculosis. Attendance increased as well. However, with the advent of antibiotics in the 1940s, which curbed the spread of tuberculosis, open-air schools disappeared by mid-century.

The Roots of Environmental Education

There was a notable interest in hiking and outdoor recreation in the early 1900s as more people had leisure time and could now travel by rail or automobile. There were a growing number of state and federal parks, though they were not equally accessible to everyone. In 1924, under the direction of President Calvin Coolidge, the first National Conference on Outdoor Recreation convened. Its aim was to coordinate national policies related to outdoor recreation, with a secondary goal to promote conservation of natural resources, given the influx in their usage by the public. In 1933, during the Great Depression, President Franklin Roosevelt's New Deal created a Civilian Conservation Corps (CCC) to provide jobs and implement a range of infrastructure upgrades to outdoor recreation areas. They planted trees, established campgrounds, built trails, and improved wildlife habitats. The CCC also built roads, bridges, and dams. President Roosevelt went on to enact a sweeping vision to connect national parks with historic sites, national memorials, and cemeteries.

As the century churned on, many more authors and conservationists examined the need for children to experience nature as essential to their development. Several significant books fueled the urgent need to address interactions between people and the natural world. *The Quiet Crisis* (Sears 1964) and Rachel Carson's *Silent Spring* (1962) both sounded alarms about the devastating environmental impacts of industrialization and habitat loss. These works underscored the need for environmental protections and urged greater accountability on the part of corporations, manufacturers, and businesses. Shortly thereafter, *The Sense of Wonder* was published, which provided intimate examples of time in nature with Carson's nephew (Carson 1965). Notably, Carson stated, "If a child is to keep alive his inborn sense of wonder . . . he needs the companionship of at least one adult who can share it, rediscovering with him the joy, excitement, and mystery of the world we live in" (Carson & Pratt 1998, 55). These books were powerful examples of why people must act for the sake of future generations, and they helped make the case for what would become known as environmental education.

A new age of environmental consciousness influenced far-reaching action. Under President Richard Nixon, the Environmental Education Act became law in 1970. This, combined with the establishment of Earth Day and passage of the Clean Air Act (1970) and Clean Water Act (1972), led to a new thrust for environmental education (Carter & Simmons 2010).

A child digs with a shovel during a Forest Days session with preschoolers in Falls Church, Virginia.

CREDIT: FALLS CHURCH—MCLEAN CHILDREN'S CENTER.

Indigenous Lands, Injustice, and Land Acknowledgements

Many communities attempt to honor Indigenous peoples through land acknowledgements seek to raise awareness in the greater community of the injustices perpetrated on Indigenous peoples when their land was taken through broken treaties and deceptive laws, causing generations of harm and displacement from their ancestral homes. Indigenous peoples are stewards of the land on which they live. They have a symbiotic relationship to their land that is manifest through their language and cultural heritage and their spiritual connection to nature. Indigenous peoples the world over continue to fight for land that is sacred to them. The effects of their fight are continually felt throughout Indigenous communities of North America and have a significant impact on children and families in early care environments.

We must underscore that the push for environmental education was not isolated but rather intricately part of other major issues of racial and social justice, just as it is today. As our nation continues to grapple with big questions surrounding social justice, diversity, equity, and inclusion, questions remain about who can freely and safely access nature and reap the resulting benefits.

Carl Anthony, an early environmental justice leader, worked to tackle these issues. In 1990 he founded the first journal devoted to environmental justice, *Race, Poverty, and the Environment*. Through grassroots community-based initiatives, Anthony helped raise awareness of the unique environmental challenges that disproportionately impact impoverished communities and communities of color. While many of these issues still permeate the systems and organizations that guide environmental action and education, Anthony and others were early proponents for environmental justice.

The Growth of Environmental Education

The North American Association of Environmental Education (NAAEE) defines *environmental education* as "a process that helps individuals, communities, and organizations learn more about the environment, and to develop skills and understanding about how to address global challenges" (Hollweg et al. 2011). This definition refers to the importance of addressing social equity, environmental integrity, and shared prosperity to ensure a more harmonious, sustainable future (World Commission on Environment and Development 1987). Environmental education, as it exists in the current educational landscape, is an experiential and interdisciplinary approach that focuses on problem solving and citizen engagement to address the social and environmental issues at hand (Hollweg et al. 2011). *Environmental literacy* is an outcome of environmental education. Environmentally literate people are educated about environmental issues and act to positively preserve, conserve, or effect change in the environment. NAAEE's *Developing a Framework for the Assessment of Environmental Literacy* states:

> An environmentally literate person, both individually and together with others, makes informed decisions concerning the environment; is willing to act on these decisions to improve the well-being of other individuals, societies, and the global environment; and participates in civic life. Those who are environmentally literate possess, to varying degrees:
>
> › Knowledge and understanding of a wide range of environmental concepts, problems, and issues;
>
> › A set of cognitive and affective dispositions;
>
> › A set of cognitive skills and abilities;
>
> › The appropriate behavioral strategies to apply such knowledge and understanding in order to make sound and effective decisions in a range of environmental contexts. (Hollweg et al. 2011, 6)

Nature-based education incorporates developmentally appropriate experiences to promote environmental literacy, making environmental education an undercurrent that directly informs the work of nature-based educators. Children actively make decisions and participate in caretaking that supports values of environmental literacy and nature-based learning—for example, by composting their food waste and planting native flowers to support local bee populations.

There is no agreement about precisely when the term "environmental education" came into use, but many credit Jean-Jacques Rousseau's 1762 book *Emile, or a Treatise on Education*. Rousseau made the first known reference, asserting that learning should include a focus on nature following the child's direction. He also discussed the value of facilitating learning experiences that allow children to discover information rather than memorizing facts, which is a concept that continues in modern nature pedagogy (Carter & Simmons 2010).

Children create a shelter to protect animals and call it "Animal House" at Epiphany Preschool in Vienna, Virginia.

CREDIT: EPIPHANY PRESCHOOL.

Similarly, the term "outdoor education" can be relevant to nature-based learning. An early definition appears in *Outdoor Education: Definition and Philosophy*, by Phyllis Ford and published by the Office of Educational Research and Development, which describes outdoor education as being "in, about, and/or the out of doors" (Ford 1986). Sound familiar? Ford outlines precepts that closely mirror many of the goals of environmental education. Yet, Ford explains that outdoor education also includes a wide range of outdoor activities that take place during leisure time purely for pleasure or some other intrinsic value, including hiking, swimming, boating, winter sports, cycling, and camping. For this reason, outdoor education is sometimes viewed as casual experiences outdoors, although the term "outdoor recreation" may prove the better descriptor for those activities. Today we apply the term outdoor education to encompass all kinds of learning that takes place outdoors, inclusive of environmental education.

The Affordances of Nature for Early Childhood Learning

The experiences made possible in outdoor settings are dynamic and rich when compared with classroom-bound learning. Consider the physical restrictions on how children must use their voices and their bodies, as well as the lack of movement on a given day when learning in a classroom. Learning is often seated at a table or on the floor, and talking must be with inside voices. Running is typically not allowed, except during designated times for large motor play. Research underscores the concerns about the lack of movement and sedentary time in many school programs, even those offered to preschool-age children. (Hanscom 2016; Wiseman et al. 2019). In contrast, when children are outdoors, they have opportunities to run, roll, spin, climb, jump, and skip. They master their locomotor and gross motor skills, which is not only wonderful for physical development but can also reduce obesity rates (Dyment & Bell 2008; Fjørtoft 2004). Similarly, children can talk loudly, call to friends, sing, call out, and make all manner of sounds as they engage in outdoor play. Being in natural outdoor play spaces also encourages greater use of expressive and receptive language and imaginative play, and complements goals of social and emotional development overall (Dankiw et al. 2020; Kuo et al. 2019). Nature-based experiences can happen indoors with natural materials and artifacts, but nothing replaces the direct experience of nature play in outdoor settings.

The following benefits are "10 Reasons Kids Need Outdoor Learning," published by the Association for Nature-Based Education in 2024:

1. **Fresh air:** There's more oxygen in the air outdoors, so you can literally think better outside.
2. **Sunshine:** It gives bodies a boost of vitamin D, which is essential for healthy immune systems and is linked with the healthy development of eyes.
3. **Soil:** Mycobacterium vaccae, a naturally occurring bacteria in soil, produces calming effects that can improve cognition and memory.
4. **Grit:** Physical and emotional risk-taking requires determination, builds confidence, and instills perseverance.
5. **Resourcefulness:** Natural materials are often plentiful and free and hold endless potential when in a child's hands.
6. **Wonder:** Weird, amazing, beautiful, and gross things happen in nature. Wonder, curiosity, and awe are fantastic intrinsic motivators for learning.
7. **Trial and error:** Science inquiry and experimentation unfolds in every season.
8. **Collaboration:** Open-ended exploration invites social play, teamwork, communication, and problem solving with others.
9. **Strong Bodies:** Learning is less restrictive outdoors and is inherently more active. Movement and motor planning are linked with improved cognitive skills and lower rates of obesity.
10. **Connectedness:** We are part of a shared experience on the land. We contribute to the harmony of our communities, both natural and human. As we grow to know nature, we learn to love and care for it.

These and other benefits of nature contact for children are also described in a 2015 study of the same name (Chawla & Nasar 2015).

These benefits also hold true for children in low-income communities when they engage in nature-based programs at public schools. In addition, children demonstrate significant gains in STEM-based learning in rural, suburban, and urban schools when nature-based learning and play are incorporated into the curriculum (Sprague & Ekenga 2020). The benefits of nature-based education will be discussed in depth in Chapter 1.

What Is Nature-Based Early Childhood Education?

In nature-based education, children develop an affinity for the special aspects of their native (local) landscape. They form bonds with the physical space and discover local traditions, past and present. For example, on the coast of Delaware Bay, families may gather to watch the horseshoe crabs lay eggs under a full moon every May. In Montana, children may learn to identify and ethically harvest huckleberries for jam or tea. In Oklahoma, the Kentucky coffee tree can be a source of legumes that once roasted can be eaten with homemade ice cream. In Washington state, children may learn about a kettle of Swainson's hawks returning in spring. Respect and active participation in the community is a natural outgrowth of this understanding, which cultivates a strong sense of place (Sobel 2013). Real-world problem solving and learning as part of the community bring appreciation for the places where children grow and learn.

Unique in its focus compared to environmental education or outdoor education, nature pedagogy within the framework of early childhood education embraces nature as the platform for all teaching and foundational learning, which nurtures the bond between child and nature. Every aspect of this holistic teaching method—from curriculum and learning environments to teaching practices and community engagement—supports healthy growth and child development. Nature pedagogy is significantly distinguished from traditional early childhood pedagogy, however, because it is rooted in direct experiences that take place

Children explore the shoreline at Miami Nature Playschool in Miami, Florida.

CREDIT: MIAMI NATURE PLAYSCHOOL.

in, about, with, and for nature. Traits of resourcefulness, empathy, gratitude, kindness, creativity, confidence, and determination blossom with nature pedagogy as the backdrop of early learning.

Long-standing academic research tells us that our formative experiences are shaped by parents, family, peers, community, culture, environment, and interactions between them. Learning constantly unfolds in the context of the child's genetic conditions and these evolving relationships. When these influential components are examined through the lens of NBECE, we reveal the potential for children to tap into places they intimately know as home.

Simply put, NBECE combines an understanding of developmentally appropriate practices in early childhood education with the precepts of environmental education and unfettered nature play. NBECE embraces emergent learning that arises in nature as children engage in child-directed learning—both of which are essential to meaningful connection with the natural world. "Emergent learning" in this context refers to children's spontaneous interests and explorations sparked by playful, unplanned interactions that are plentiful in every season. NBECE honors diversity and culture through place-based experiences on the land and in community with one another. It is inclusive and celebrates the dynamic backgrounds and experiences of young children. As you will see, NBECE provides an ideal approach to holistic learning in early childhood (Kuo et al. 2019).

Children discover local plants and animals, which is especially satisfying in their own gardens.

CREDIT: MONTESSORI LUNA BILINGUAL MICRO SCHOOL, PIKESVILLE, MARYLAND.

Over the last two decades, an outpouring of research and writing has helped articulate just what NBECE is. Mary Rivkin, Bora Simmons, David Sobel, Ken Finch, Patti Bailie, Claire Warden, Erin Kenny, Jon Young, Marty Watson, Rachel Larimore, Yash Bashwanji, Ruth Wilson, Sara Knight, Ellen Sandseter, Julia Torquati, Tim Gill, Julie Ernst, Louise Chawla, and Sheila Williams Ridge are but a few contemporary leaders to note. They have shared their experiences working directly with young children in outdoor settings and provided writing, research, and tools to develop best practices around NBECE. Given more time, a survey of their work would prove useful, but one cannot frame NBECE without making mention of their contributions, some of which are cited here.

As a result of these contributions and wonderful examples of nature-based programs, an educational movement has swelled, giving rise to what naturalists (people who study nature) and early childhood practitioners have come to recognize as NBECE (NAAEE 2017). Many people credit Richard Louv's book *Last Child in the Woods: Saving Our Children from Nature-Deficit Disorder* as the harbinger that gave wings to nature-based programs the world over (Louv 2008).

Examples of Nature-Based Early Childhood Education Programs

As varied as early childhood environments can be, NBECE exists in just as many forms. It may come as no surprise that nature preschools, nature kindergartens, forest preschools, forest kindergartens, and outdoor preschools incorporate NBECE in a myriad of ways. Each term suggests a slightly different approach to NBECE:

› **Nature preschool:** Arguably the American cousin of European nature kindergartens, nature preschools are typically part- or full-day licensed programs that blend state-required standards with the goals of NBECE. They may be attached to a nature center or larger school and utilize both indoor and outdoor learning spaces (Bailie 2012).

› **Nature kindergarten:** A program that affords long blocks of play in wild, naturalistic landscapes among mixed age groups of 2 through 5 years old (Warden 2010). This term is more commonly used in Europe since the term "kindergarten" in the United States typically refers to children age 5 attending public school.

› **Forest preschool or Forest kindergarten:** Refers to a fully immersive outdoor learning program. Children ages 2 through 6 years old experience seasonal elements as integral to the learning process. The precise age range is dependent on the program, but preschool usually refers to ages 3 through 5 years old (i.e., children not yet eligible for kindergarten). Depending on the location of the forest preschool or forest kindergarten, it may be run as a licensed childcare program. In Washington state, recent legislation provides regulations to

Children investigate life on a frozen pond in Lee, New Hampshire.

CREDIT: LIVE & LEARN EARLY LEARNING CENTER.

license fully outdoor preschools (Washington State Department of Children, Youth & Families 2021). If an indoor facility can be accessed, a forest preschool may use the indoor space for licensing purposes but hold the program exclusively outside. In most cases, fully outdoor preschools cannot be licensed, therefore they may be considered a nature program, nature camp, nature club, nature play date, or some other term to denote a less formal structure.

> **Forest school and nature school:** These are also broad terms that may describe a fully immersive outdoor school program or mode of home school study. This may also refer to one component of an existing school. For example, "We're having forest school today!" suggests that learning will take place outdoors on a given day but that it is not necessarily the approach to daily learning.

Children use tools such as these mallets to explore natural materials found in local habitats, in this case, Coyle, Oklahoma.

CREDIT: PRAIRIEWOOD FOREST SCHOOL AT ST. FRANCIS OF THE WOODS.

The Forest School Association guides a large, organized system of practitioners and schools in the United Kingdom. They define Forest School as "a child-centred inspirational learning process, which offers opportunities for holistic growth through regular sessions. It is a long-term program that supports play, exploration and risk taking. It develops confidence and self-esteem through learner inspired, hands-on experiences in a natural setting" (Forest School Association, n.d.). By this definition, all of the terms listed here might be considered forest schools, depending on the implementation of their practices.

> **Forest days, nature days, outdoor learning days:** These can all refer to a special time set aside during the school day—especially in a traditional school setting—for immersive outdoor learning experiences that complement curricular goals and standards. Eliza Minnucci and Meghan Teachout give a thorough description of how to implement such programs in their book *A Forest Days Handbook: Program Design for School Days Outside* (2018).

Lastly, although these terms frequently refer to a "forest," the approach to outdoor learning is not limited to forests alone. NBECE can take place on a farm, beach, desert, mountain, marsh, jungle, park, zoo, rooftop, urban cityscape, backyard—anywhere children may be. There is no limit to where NBECE can exist because we all embody nature, and it is everywhere. With thoughtful consideration and perhaps a bit of creativity, any setting can be a place for nature-based learning.

Kindred Spirits to Nature-Based Early Childhood Education

NBECE draws from playful philosophies you may already be familiar with. Traditions in Montessori, Waldorf, and Reggio Emilia schools share common threads of learning. The following offers a little taste of each approach to help frame how nature-based learning relates. Although the curriculum is not necessarily nature based, each is a kindred spirit of NBECE and shares a love of natural materials, values independence, and supports child-directed inquiry and play, often outdoors.

Dr. Maria Montessori, founder of the Montessori Method of teaching, was a pioneering Italian doctor and early childhood educator. In this method, children are encouraged to make choices, play, and engage in hands-on learning in a carefully prepared learning environment with provisions for specific age ranges. She observed that "the child has a mind able to absorb knowledge. He has the power to teach himself" (Montessori 1995,6). To this end, Montessori asserts that when trained teachers set up the learning environment with beautiful, developmentally appropriate materials, the children easily acquire new skills through their play. Similarly, child-directed play and hands-on learning are prominent in NBECE programs, but it is nature that provides materials for children to interact with in NBECE programs.

Children are physically active when engaged in outdoor play. Here children boost their endurance and grit as they trudge uphill in Baltimore, Maryland.

CREDIT: THE WALDORF SCHOOL OF BALTIMORE.

Waldorf education was established by Austrian artist and scientist Rudolph Steiner. The first school opened in 1919 in Germany, largely in opposition to the regimented, teacher-directed approaches of the school system during that time. His progressive philosophy includes hands-on learning that appeals to the tendencies of children at various stages in their development. For young children, Steiner notes that imitation, empathy, and experience are essential to a holistic approach to curricula. Waldorf schools welcome creative and imaginative play alongside practical learning such as baking and sweeping. Steiner noted, "The need for imagination, a sense of truth, and a feeling of responsibility, these are the three forces which are the very nerves of pedagogy" (Steiner 1919). By comparison, NBECE also emphasizes empathy as a way to form deep connections with the natural world and relationships among the learning community. Tool use, foraging, and handcrafts are examples of practical skills children learn in nature-based programs. Open-ended nature play also provides an outlet for hands-on learning and imaginative play, dovetailing with Steiner's vision of early childhood education.

Reggio Emilia, Italy, is the birthplace of the Reggio Emilia Approach to learning. Founder Loris Malaguzzi envisioned a philosophy of learning whereby teachers co-collaborate to develop curriculum with children, observing and documenting the learning processes to make learning visible. In this philosophy, children explore their own questions through an open-ended, project-based approach. In his poem "The Hundred Languages of Children," Malaguzzi offers a beautiful description of the diverse capacity children have for learning (Edwards et al. 2012): "The hundred languages are a metaphor for the extraordinary potentials of children, their knowledge-building and creative processes, the myriad forms with which life is manifested, and knowledge is constructed" (Reggio Children, n.d.). This fierce protection of children as capable, independent thinkers resonates with nature-based educators. The role of the teacher as a facilitator who provokes and stimulates learning rather than as a didactic teacher is another commonality between the Reggio Emilia Approach and NBECE. Furthermore, the importance of the learning process and its documentation are also applied in both contexts.

Challenges to Equitable Nature-Based Learning

Because people are part of the natural world, it stands to reason that nature-based learning is available to everyone. But this hasn't been the case for many children. As nature-based programs take root alongside other environmental initiatives, we must be careful that they don't inadvertently "reinforce inequalities or lead to new forms of social exclusion" (Tozer et al. 2020). Children whose families live at or below the poverty level face disproportionate challenges when it comes to attendance in nature-based programs.

Experiential learning is the best way for children to develop nature connection, like this child at Notchcliff Nature Programs, which is the lab forest school for the Association for Nature-Based Education in Glen Arm, Maryland.

CREDIT: ASSOCIATION FOR NATURE-BASED EDUCATION, NOTCHCLIFF NATURE PROGRAMS.

A national study conducted in 2017 by the Natural Start Alliance, with partners from the Eastern Region Association of Forest and Nature Schools, the Washington Nature Preschool Association, and the Northern Illinois Nature Preschool Association, revealed extreme disparities among the participants of nature-based programs. The survey notes that 83 percent of children in nature-based programs were White, suggesting barriers to equitable access (NAAEE 2017).

This is shocking, considering census data shows that less than 50 percent of children under age 5 in the United States are non-Hispanic White (Frey 2019). The survey also found that less than 5 percent of children received special education services or were dual language learners, yet nationally 13 percent of children receive special education services, and nearly one-fifth of all American children live in a dual language household (Frey 2019; NAAEE 2017).

We mentioned previously that licensing of immersive nature-based programs is not available in all states, which is a significant contributing factor to equitable access for all children, particularly those who need financial assistance and specialized services to attend. These are challenges that NBECE practitioners and advocates are working diligently to address to ensure all children can reap the benefits of nature-based learning.

Here are some of the most pressing considerations:

› *Cost:* Are programs free or offered on a sliding scale? Is financial assistance available either from the school or state subsidies? Can every family afford to attend?

› *Hours of operation:* Can families with two full-time working parents or families with one single working parent realistically receive care if they want to attend these programs?

› *Location:* Do families need a car to attend? Are programs located within walking distance of public transportation?

› *Safety:* Is there crime, pollution, traffic, or other safety concerns in the immediate area?

› *Representation:* Does staff diversity reflect children in the community and those you would like to serve?

› *Gear and supplies:* If families cannot afford materials or gear, is there a discrete way for families to receive what they need?

› *Services:* If children require special education services, does your program know how to obtain them for every child?

› *Social stigma and fear:* People of Color have historically been targeted as criminals when recreating outdoors (Finney 2014; Powers et al. 2024; Roberts 2015). Does your program advocate overcoming these stereotypes and forming trusting relationships in the community?

Which of these considerations are you currently facing? These important questions and challenges are examined in detail in Chapter 5.

Bilingual Learning at Forest School

By Pilar Gonzalez, Founding Director, Aventuras Forest School, Los Angeles, California

At Aventuras Forest School, Southern California's first Spanish immersion forest school, we plan themes loosely and flexibly to follow the seasons and holidays, what we observe in our surroundings, and what interests the children. One spring, we were observing a lot of nesting activity in the park where we hold school, so we decided to do a theme

Autumn leaves are perfect to inspire sorting by size, shape, or color, as seen here.

CREDIT: MONICA WIEDEL-LUBINSKI.

on birds. We borrowed children's books in Spanish from the library about birds, nesting, and spring and read them as we ate lunch, picnic-style. When we read books, we usually do a quick introduction in English to support the comprehension of the English-dominant children, then we read the rest of the book in Spanish using gestures, pictures, and real-world objects to further support their comprehension.

During one story time as we were reading in Spanish about how birds build nests, we observed some unusual activity. A bird was flying repeatedly between one area near a tree on one side of us, to a cavity in another tree on the other side of us, holding something in its mouth. We saw the bird go back and forth many times like this. We hypothesized that the bird may have been lining its nest in a cavity of a tree or perhaps feeding insects to its young. The kids were extremely excited to have the book virtually come to life before their eyes. After lunch, the children decided spontaneously to collect sticks in their environment and build small nests, pretending to be birds, further enriching their learning and having fun at the same time.

This experience illustrates some of the many ways that experiential outdoor learning has been so rich and effective for teaching young children at Aventuras. By watching the bird's behavior and guessing the reasons for it, they were learning the important scientific inquiry skills of observing and making hypotheses. The children are naturally curious about animals and other things they encounter in a real-world, outdoor setting, so they need only the slightest encouragement from their teachers to notice their environment, ask questions, and form theories about the world around them.

As we were reading about birds and nesting, the children also learned the vocabulary and concepts more easily because they were engaged through multiple senses and real objects rather than just hearing a vocabulary word or reading a book in isolation. We see this kind of learning all the time—whether our students spot an awesome-looking object and learn that it's a praying mantis egg case or can identify a small rodent by estimating its size and looking it up in our field guide, they eagerly learn the names and characteristics of what they are seeing in the natural world.

When free to use their imaginations, the children come up with their own way to deepen understanding. Child-directed play lets them experiment with new ideas and concepts and make them their own. At the beginning of the COVID-19 pandemic, we heard many stories about children incorporating masked stuffed animals into their play. This allowed them to make sense of their world, internalize new learning, and explore their feelings in a safe space. At Aventuras, we see every day how play-based learning is the most fundamentally human way for children to learn.

As the research and benefits of NBECE become more widely publicized, traditional licensed preschools, childcare centers, and in-home childcare providers are also integrating NBECE into their programs.

NBECE embodies the ideals of nature pedagogy by combining best practices of early childhood education, environmental education, and nature play. The result is a union of responsive, developmentally appropriate practices and nature connection. Children grow gratitude, empathy, and respect for themselves and the natural world as they develop foundation skills across social, emotional, physical, and cognitive domains.

Experiential learning is the best way for children to develop nature connection, like this child at Notchcliff Nature Programs, which is the lab forest school for the Association for Nature-Based Education (ANBE) in Glen Arm, Maryland.

CREDIT: ASSOCIATION FOR NATURE-BASED EDUCATION, NOTCHCLIFF NATURE PROGRAMS.

Appendix: Why Do We Connect with Nature?

Two important concepts have emerged to explain our longing for nature connection. First, the term *topophilia* refers to "the affective bond between people and place or setting" as described by Yi-Fu Tuan, who is considered a key figure in human geography or the study of how humans and human communities relate to and interact with their environment (Kirk 1975, 7700). He pointed to the complexities of aesthetic design that impact everything from travel and leisure to how we care for our backyards. He also believed that the converse, topophobia, also exists. Just as people can have strong ties to the environment, they may also have an intense dislike or fear of it.

Second, E.O. Wilson offered the *biophilia hypothesis*, which expands to some extent on topophilia (Wilson 1984). Wilson was an American biologist and natural scientist who founded the E.O. Wilson Foundation for the study of biodiversity, or how all animals and humans interact (https://eowilsonfoundation.org/about-us/e-o-wilson). He reasoned that people have an innate desire to connect with other living things, and a preference for natural environments (Kahn 1999; Kellert & Wilson 1993; Wilson 1984). Furthermore, Kellert and Wilson (1993) describe nine overarching biophilic values people demonstrate to varying degrees, which help frame the evolutionary basis for each of the values. When we work with young children, these values are rapidly emerging and easy to observe.

Table A.1 Biophilic Values with Descriptions

Biophilic Value	Description	Example
Utilitarian	Nature has material value because it is useful; nature provides humans with sustenance, protection, and security.	People find rare or abundant sources of food, medicine, clothing, tools, and precious gems in nature. Resources in nature are utilized but may be exploited for financial advantage or gain.
Naturalistic	Satisfaction is derived from direct contact with nature; nature's diversity and complexities are appreciated; observation, discovery, and exploration of living diversity is possible in nature.	People experience fascination, wonder, and awe in nature. Curiosity and a desire to explore nature may also lead to physical fitness and acquisition of outdoor skills. Contact with nature can provide stress relief, peace, and enhanced creativity.

Biophilic Value	Description	Example
Ecologistic-scientific	Nature can be studied through systematic inquiry, investigation, and analysis of the natural world. Ecology and science lead to knowledge about structures that make up complex systems of interconnection and interdependence in nature.	Specific aspects of nature can be explored such as food chains, energy pyramids, biotic and abiotic relationships, flow of energy from the sun, pollination, and seed dispersal. This knowledge can lead to deeper appreciation but can also result in exploitation, mimicry, or abuse of natural processes and species if only considered in isolation rather than in relationship to the whole.
Aesthetic	Physical beauty and the vitality of nature are appreciated. Natural designs and patterns are preferred. Animals within the landscape are aesthetically appreciated.	People appreciate nature's harmony, symmetry, and order. Aesthetic appreciation may include feelings of tranquility, peace, and related self-confidence. This relates to a genetic need for pattern, harmony, and beauty as a result of natural selection for survival.
Symbolic	Nature is a means of facilitating communication and thought, reflected in the development of human language.	Acquisition of language is enhanced by categories and distinctions mirrored in nature; habit of symbolizing in terms of animals with significance in myths, fairy tales, and stories.
Humanistic	Feelings of deep emotional attachment to elements of the natural world; enhanced capacity for bonding, altruism, and sharing.	Feelings of attachment for a particular animal, tree, or stone. Feelings of "love" toward nature or pets; therapeutic benefits of companion animals; care and nurturing of individual elements of nature.
Moralistic	Strong feelings of affinity, ethical responsibility, and reverence for nature; ethical and spiritual connectedness with nature; reciprocity between humans and nature; link between human identity and the natural landscape.	Fundamental belief in the natural world as a living and vital being; helping behavior and a desire to protect and conserve; sense of well-being, identity, and confidence for those with conviction of the ultimate order and meaning of life.
Dominionistic	Desire to master the natural world; capacity to subdue or dominate forces of nature.	Struggle to survive brings about a keen awareness of nature and the need to dominate it for survival (e.g., predator-prey relationships).
Negativistic	Fear, aversion, or antipathy toward nature.	Behaviors and attitudes that reject threatening aspects of nature; active escape and avoidance that can lead to unwarranted harm or destruction.

> **CALL TO ACTION**
>
> Find forest or nature schools in your area and schedule a tour. As you observe, note how the indoor and outdoor learning environments are arranged and utilized.

Reflection Questions

- What are the key historical factors that led to the formation of NBECE?
- What are the seven principles of NBECE?
- How do these principles relate to you or your program's approach to outdoor learning?

CHAPTER 2

Child Development and the Benefits of Nature-Based Learning

When teachers offer time, space, and permission for children to engage in nature-based learning, the positive benefits span a wide range of developmental domains and values. This magical (and essential) trifecta opens up possibilities for nature connection through unhurried inquiry and discovery. This chapter emphasizes the many benefits of nature-based learning, with a focus on children being outdoors.

Guiding Questions:

As you read through this chapter, consider the following questions:

- What sensory experiences are the favorites in your program? How are they related to nature or natural materials?

- How can nature-based activities or experiences support physical development in your program?

- Considering social and emotional skills, what nature-based group activities could enhance your curriculum, especially during outdoor play?

- Compare your existing literacy activities with examples offered for nature-based language development. What are three activities or experiences that could scaffold with what you currently do?

- Are there barriers for children to engage fully with nature? If there are, consider what layered approach you can implement to address these barriers within your learning community.

Supporting Developmental Domains

NOTE: *"Developmental domains" are described differently by various researchers, and they are classified differently from state to state. Domains may include different categories such as Language/Communication, Self-Help/Adaptive Skills, Social-Emotional, Physical Development and Health, and Spiritual Development. Sometimes content areas such as math and science are listed as developmental domains. Here we refer to NAEYC's description of developmental domains as our point of reference (NAEYC 2020).*

Physical Development

Children can spread their wings outside! They have greater freedom of movement outdoors, which means they can engage in more physically active play when compared with indoor environments. By contrast, there is increasing concern about the amount of time children are engaged in sedentary activities at home, at school, and during transit, which contributes to rising childhood obesity rates (Larouche et al. 2016; Martin et al. 2022; Schmutz et al. 2017; Tonge et al. 2024). Lack of physical activity is also correlated with an increase in screen time and extends to younger and younger children (Robinson et al. 2017).

The Mayo Clinic elaborates on the harmful impacts of too much screen time, citing obesity, irregular sleep, behavioral problems, impaired academic performance, violence, and less time for play (Brumm 2021; Valen 2023, 20). The American Academy of Pediatrics discourages any form of screen time for children under age 2 and suggests no more than one hour of daily screen time for children ages 2 to 5 years old (American Academy of Pediatrics 2023; Pappas 2022). Despite these recommendations, the average screen time for preschoolers is nearly three times as much, at 2½ to 3 hours per day (Walsh et al. 2020).

Fortunately, nature-based education offers a solution. Outdoor play keeps kids active and moving, which is a much-needed benefit to promote healthy physical child development. Outdoor environments are ripe with opportunities to develop gross and locomotor skills through hiking, climbing, running, jumping, raking, and other activities. Nature-based learning specifically promotes the development of fine motor skills when children pick up small natural objects such

Children use tools such as shovels and wheelbarrows during active nature play.

CREDIT: BLUESTONE VILLAGE AND NATURE PROGRAMS, SHOHOLA, PENNSYLVANIA.

as seeds, pebbles, or flower petals and manipulate them during play (for example, gathering, tying knots, weaving, peeling bark, or holding an ant). Children use tools to support inquiry, which also helps promote fine and gross motor skill development—for example, stirring, cutting, using a hand drill or mallet, whittling, or digging.

As children play outdoors, they often incorporate plentiful loose parts found in nature. Here, evergreens, twigs, and leaves become part of sand sculpture.

CREDIT: FALLS CHURCH–MCLEAN CHILDREN'S CENTER.

Developing the Senses

Outdoor play is also full of sensory-rich experiences. Children may **see** white-tailed deer in a meadow or notice a red-shouldered hawk on a street lamppost. They may observe brightly colored toadstool mushrooms or watch dragonflies dart across a pond, or they may delight in a snow-covered cityscape or a bird's nest under the eaves of a tall building. Children may note the tiniest color shifts in one flower petal or focus on patterns of veining on a leaf. They may notice bright yellow dandelions dotting cracks along the sidewalk or the vibrant purple crocus coming up in spring. They may get a fresh perspective watching clouds or looking down while sitting on a branch after climbing a tree (visual sense).

Children may **smell** lemony spicebush leaves, stinky skunk cabbage, sweet milkweed flowers, white pine needles, or inhale the scent of fresh rain. They may smell onion grass, catch a whiff of decaying leaves in a pond, or breathe in the scent of magnolia blossoms. Perhaps children will notice when it "smells like it's going to snow" (olfactory sense).

Children may **hear** geese honking overhead, woodpeckers tapping on trees, and the calls of birds, frogs, or insects. They may hear creaking tree trunks in gentle winds or busy squirrels rustling leaf litter. Water flowing in a brook, crackling autumn leaves, snow crunching underfoot, or humming bees are but a few of nature's sounds (auditory sense).

Children may forage to **taste** ripe berries, leaves, and flowers, eat root vegetables, taste maple sap, or make wild teas. They may enjoy fruits of a seasonal harvest like apples or corn, sample nectar from honeysuckle flowers, or taste ripened seeds and nuts. From garden-grown foods and herbs to responsibly foraged edibles, there are many ways to experience nature through the sense of taste (gustatory sense).

Children may **touch** rough grooves on tree bark or wet dew in the grass, feel a smooth acorn or the silky touch of a crow feather, or feel warmth radiate from a campfire or the sun on their brow.

Children may feel soft moss under their toes, feel the tickle of a crawling beetle, or touch the fluffy pith of a seed (tactile sense). Perhaps they touch sticky pine sap or the frost melting on a blade of grass.

There is a feast for the senses waiting outside! While most people are familiar with the five senses just described, others are less familiar with proprioceptive, vestibular, and interoceptive senses, all of which are essential for people to orient and adapt to their surroundings.

The **proprioceptive** sense sends signals that help feel where the body is in relation to other parts of the body. This happens as information is sent from muscles, ligaments, and joints to the brain (Blythe 2017). When the brain interprets this sensory input, we can determine our body position and motion. This determination helps the body adjust the amount of force needed to accomplish a given movement. For example, if a child finds a robin's eggshell on the ground, they must determine the amount of pressure to use to accurately pick it up without breaking it. Outdoor play that involves resistance, such as lifting heavy stones or logs, helps children strengthen joints, muscles, and connective tissues, which builds coordination and refines proprioceptive skills (Hanscom 2016).

The **vestibular** sense, sometimes called the "balance sense," is just that. Fluid in the inner ear helps determine balance, giving a physical awareness of one's body moving in space. A strong vestibular sense promotes coordination and body awareness. Angela Hanscom, a pediatric occupational therapist, offers insight in her book *Balanced and Barefoot: How Unrestricted Outdoor Play Makes for Strong, Confident, and Capable Children*. She elaborates on the vestibular sense, stating that "children will benefit immensely by going upside down, spinning, tumbling, and swinging" and "going upside down on the monkey bars, rolling down hills, and

Child touches soft moss growing on a rock.

CREDIT: LIVE & LEARN EARLY LEARNING CENTER, LEE, NEW HAMPSHIRE.

This child savors the whole-body experience of making a snow angel while sweeping arms and legs to move the snow.

dancing until their little hearts are content" (Hanscom 2016). Balance is a basic skill needed for children to control their bodies, and outdoor exploration is full of opportunities to refine the vestibular sense.

The sense of **interoception** may be more commonly considered similar to a gut feeling, and science tells us that there are physiological reasons our bodies have this important sense. The STAR Institute for Sensory Processing describes interoception as the "ability to perceive and understand your internal sensations, like hunger, thirst, the need to use the bathroom, feeling hot or cold, and fatigue" (Ochsenbein 2024; STAR Institute for Sensory Processing 2024). Interoception is also linked to self-regulation and interpretation of our body's physiological feelings as emotions. When we are tuned into how our bodies feel internally, we are better prepared to understand social and environmental situations and act on those sensations. There is a subconscious aspect to interoception (meaning our body automatically monitors how we are feeling) as well as ways to become more conscious and intentional about monitoring physiological cues from this sense.

Tree climbing engages core muscles along with multiple senses, including the vestibular and proprioception senses.

CREDIT: THE WALDORF SCHOOL OF BALTIMORE, MARYLAND.

Quite literally, **sensory integration** is how the brain organizes sensory input to accurately interpret information from the physical world. Dr. Jean Ayers laid the foundation to better understand the neurobiology of human behavior and neuroscience at work as our bodies process information through the senses. The theory and practice of Ayers Sensory Integration (ASI) "emphasizes the active, dynamic sensory-motor processes that support movement as well as interaction within social and physical environments and that act as a catalyst for development" (Lane et al. 2019, 1).

As evidenced in these examples, nature-based learning offers varied opportunities for sensory integration of stimuli across the eight sensory systems: visual, auditory, olfactory, gustatory, tactile, proprioceptive, vestibular, and interoceptive (Awalludin 2020; Ayres 1972; Schmitt & Schoen 2022). Nature-based programs spend time outdoors, many of them immersed in nature all day, every day, so children experience all kinds of weather, temperatures, and seasons with their whole being as part of a typical nature-based curriculum. The lived experience of adapting to the weather provides ongoing opportunities for sensory integration, as does hands-on interactions with natural materials.

Nourishing Our Bodies

When the curriculum includes gardening, growing food, or foraging, children also benefit from improved **nutrition**. Children are more likely to eat food they grow, harvest, or cook, which can lead to positive attitudes toward healthy whole foods. Most modern food production leaves people far removed from the origins of their food: Where did that peach come from, anyhow? When children are active participants in growing, tending, and harvesting food, they develop a deeper understanding of our reliance on nature for sustenance. They also benefit from eating vitamin-rich, nutritious foods, often for the first time as freshly picked produce or herbs.

We must also consider nutrition as an outgrowth of our relationship with the land and local community. The experience of gardening as a community opens up social and cultural aspects of growing food—if not for survival, then with a shared goal to help feed one another. When we consider the historical impact of colonization on Indigenous and enslaved people, it becomes clear why many people characterize colonial practices as the cause of a breakdown of Indigenous food systems. This underscores the importance of place-based approaches that honor local culture and traditions, which include growing, tending, and harvesting food (Bagelman 2018). You may not realize the diverse array of cultural traditions among your learning community. Inviting families to plant a garden can reveal many exciting aspects of culture to share and celebrate, often in the form of beloved recipes.

Caring for plants is another way to engage a range of senses and skills.

CREDIT: MONTESSORI LUNA BILINGUAL MICRO SCHOOL, PIKESVILLE, MARYLAND.

Children's bodies also benefit from nutrients derived from sunlight, soil, and fresh air. Vitamin D is unique in that our skin produces a vitamin D hormone in response to sunlight (Aboulghar et al. 2021). When people spend time outdoors, they naturally absorb vitamin D from the sun. In addition to bone health, vitamin D is linked to many positive effects that protect us from chronic illness and disease.

Playing in the soil and breathing fresh air are also inherently beneficial. The soil contains healthy bacteria called mycobacterium, and studies show that some strains have anti-inflammatory, immunoregulatory, and stress-resilience properties. More outdoor time can also mean that kids inhale fewer indoor air pollutants and instead take in higher levels of oxygen. (This benefit

Most forest and nature schools incorporate campfire cooking into their programs.

CREDIT: ASSOCIATION FOR NATURE-BASED EDUCATION, NOTCHCLIFF NATURE PROGRAMS.

varies based on location, and there are many considerations around equitable access to safe soil and air quality.) An abundance of research indicates that time outdoors is an excellent way to improve cognition, with positive effects following time spent outside (Bailey & Kang 2022; Goblirsch 2023; Wyver 2024). With all the active play that occurs outdoors, children experience a greater flow of oxygen-rich blood that improves brain function.

Another added benefit of outdoor play is improved vision. Eyes adjust to natural sunlight and absorb vitamin D, which some studies point to as having a protective effect against myopia (or nearsightedness). One recent study states that "both very early childhood exposure to fixed and mobile screen devices and a lower level of outdoor activity were associated with the later preschool myopia, and outdoor activity moderated the influence of screen use particularly for children whose parents were myopic"

> **Place-based education** (PBE) is a teaching method that uses the local community and environment as the foundation to teach concepts across the curriculum (Cox 2024). Renowned author and educator David Sobel explains that place-based education "teaches about both the natural and built environments" as well as the "history, folk culture, social problems, economics, and aesthetics of the community and its environment" (Sobel 2005, 9).
>
> PBE elaborates on environmental education by emphasizing the importance of active knowledge and care for the local community. In his book *Place-Based Education: Connecting Classrooms and Communities*, Sobel explains that it is:
>
> > . . . the process of using the local community and environment as a starting point to teach concepts in language arts, mathematics, social studies, science and other subjects across the curriculum. Emphasizing hands-on, real-world learning experiences, this approach to education increases academic achievement, helps students develop stronger ties to their community, enhances students' appreciation for the natural world, and creates a heightened commitment to serving as active, contributing citizens. Community vitality and environmental quality are improved through the active engagement of local citizens, community organizations, and environmental resources in the life of the school (Sobel 2005, 7).

(Huang et al. 2021, 11). This study was conducted among twenty-six thousand child participants and points to very real benefits for eye health when children spend time outdoors.

Social and Emotional Development

One of the greatest advantages of nature-based education is that children have time to direct their own learning through unstructured nature play. **Nature play** is intrinsically motivated, child-directed outdoor play that takes place in a natural setting or green space and involves interaction with natural elements or features (Dankiw et al. 2023; Ernst et al. 2021). Nature play is typically unstructured with no predetermined outcomes or structured objectives. Nature-based programs incorporate nature play into daily learning, which offers generous swaths of time for social and emotional development. Children are free to explore friendships, express and consider ideas of others, and experience the confidence that comes from making independent choices as a capable learner.

Children wash, cut, and sort fruits and vegetables before enjoying their harvest.

CREDIT: PRAIRIEWOOD FOREST SCHOOL AT ST. FRANCIS OF THE WOODS.

Perseverance

Nature-based education embraces a culture that shifts from teachers who direct every aspect of learning to children who are empowered and seen as capable of manifesting their own ideas and learning directions. There is great opportunity for problem solving and determination as children negotiate, identify solutions, and persevere through challenges encountered in outdoor settings or through the use of tools and natural materials. Perseverance is only possible if teachers don't jump in with immediate solutions and answers to problems.

NOTE: *Social and emotional domains of child development are closely linked, and while some sources categorize them separately, they can also be considered as one larger social-emotional domain. Because of the overlap, they are discussed together here.*

For some teachers, it is uncomfortable to watch children struggle to find solutions rather than giving them an immediate (adult) solution to their problem. Some teachers even feel it is their duty to help children when they struggle, which may be necessary depending on the circumstance. But this must be tempered with the understanding that if we take away the struggle in problem solving, we also remove the opportunity for the child to persevere on their own.

The term "child-directed" means that children are free to make choices about their own learning or play experiences. In child-directed, nature-based settings, children take the initiative to problem solve because they are afforded the space to do so in a learning environment that values taking time to figure things out. This unhurried approach means children can move at the pace of their own learning processes, which cultivates grit and perseverance.

Resilience

From warm breezes to icy wind, green foliage to bare trees, nature reveals changes each day. Changes can be subtle or remarkable, and we can predictably count on nature's unpredictable ways. Developing the ability to adapt to changes, big and small, is an important skill. Children become resilient when they learn how to adjust and cope with changing circumstances like those in their learning environment and daily life situations.

Changes are evident (and constant) in a natural learning environment. Consider a flock of birds taking flight overhead, a path of muddy puddles, a patch of violets in bloom, or a fresh blanket of snow. Seasonal changes provide opportunities for children to become not only more observant but also more flexible and resilient as they adjust their behavior and expectations in response to change. Novel, nature-based experiences are a wonderful way for children to approach learning—and life!—with a flexible mindset. Resilience is evident as children adapt their thinking and behavior to accept new situations as they arise, which is a key component to self-regulating emotions (Tillman et al. 2018). Nature-based learning is full of direct experiences that involve flexible thinking. Activities such as group play and problem solving (e.g., building a fort) demand the consideration of others. When children get used to adjusting to the environments and the needs of others, they become more resilient.

Jump! Children move their bodies as they engage in trail walks and outdoor exploration.

CREDIT: ASSOCIATION FOR NATURE-BASED EDUCATION, NOTCHCLIFF NATURE PROGRAMS.

This is in stark contrast to highly regimented, teacher-directed approaches to learning. Overly controlled classrooms can greatly hinder children's social and emotional development. When teachers direct exactly what children must do all day, every day, children are shortchanged. They miss out on learning how to adapt and problem solve on their own, especially in social situations. Children may have little, if any, opportunities to develop resilience in teacher-directed environments. In comparison, when kids run into unexpected challenges during nature play, such as a branch giving way causing a favorite earth shelter to crumble, or the onset of rain, coping with these bumps will ultimately help children become more resilient as they learn how to adapt and solve their own problems.

When a child experiences frustration or failure, teachers need not take it personally! Many times, this is precisely what needs to happen for a child to try and try again. It is the process of *trying*, the struggle to find a workable solution, that will lead children to discover or invent an answer to the challenges they are facing. Children cannot know the personal satisfaction that comes from perseverance when a teacher swoops in to solve every problem that comes along. In turn, children cannot develop resilience if they haven't had to apply a flexible mindset and adapt to discover their own solutions.

Outdoor learning provides opportunities for children to show caring and support toward one another.

CREDIT: ASSOCIATION FOR NATURE-BASED EDUCATION, NOTCHCLIFF NATURE PROGRAMS.

Self-Confidence and Independence

As children develop habits of play around perseverance and develop resilience, they also become increasingly independent and self-confident. Forest Schools Education founder, author, and educator Sarah Blackwell conducted research to determine the impacts of forest schools on children's resilience, confidence, and overall well-being. She notes that forest schools have many positive impacts, such as greater "self efficacy, persistence and problem solving skills." She continues to note other long-term benefits on children's confidence and describes their "marked propensity to take risks, heightened levels of self belief, positive attitude, independence and increased tendency of taking initiative" (Blackwell 2015, 2).

Traits of self-confidence and independence flourish when we trust children's abilities. When we trust children to listen to their bodies and challenge themselves, they come to trust teachers and peers who provide support when they need more guidance or tools to navigate a challenge. Trusting give-and-take relationships offer a safe context for children to develop independent self-help skills and the confidence to know they can succeed.

Friendship and Cooperation

It may come as no surprise that unstructured nature play does wonders for children's social interactions with peers. With ample opportunities to choose how and when to play, children navigate social situations that help them practice entering into play, share and consider others' ideas, and work together. This holds true when children problem solve together, experience and resolve conflict, or engage in deep imaginative play.

Cultivating Values

One significant reason that parents enroll children in nature-based programs is because they want their children to become more aware of and connected with the natural world (more on this benefit later). A great deal of nature connection involves nurturing values that improve emotional intelligence.

Shelters like this one afford spaces for exploration and imaginary play.

As children have frequent, direct experiences with nature, they develop **empathy** for other things in their environment. Initially this may be talking to a small creature such as a snail with comments like, "Aww! It is so cute! Here you go, Swirly. She wants to go home to her mommy." Children relate to other living things through perspective taking; in this case, the child imagines how the snail might feel and gives it a special name. Empathy helps children relate to nature and one another with greater awareness and sensitivity, often for living and nonliving things alike.

An outgrowth of empathy is expanding to include **forgiveness** as children relate to how they feel when they have made a bad choice or upset a friend. They become more willing to forgive when they can consider how someone else may be feeling. Likewise, they come to know how it feels to be forgiven by others. **Consent** is another aspect of helping children learn that their opinions matter and they have choices about what is and is not okay in their lives. It is important and empowering for children to learn how to create, voice, and respect the boundaries of others. While forgiveness is a value that is cultivated, it is not a given.

Empathy is closely linked with another important value: compassion. **Compassion** is an active state of doing something kind to help another in need. When children feel empathy toward the elements in a natural learning environment, they are inclined to act with compassion when they see a need. For example, when it is difficult for birds to find buried food on a snowy day, children show compassion by making bird feeders and filling them with seed. Or, if one child is struggling to climb over a log, another may be quick to lend a helping hand. When we hone a personal sense of empathy for others, acts of compassion often follow.

Nature-based programs also infuse daily practices of **gratitude** to help children appreciate their life and circumstances, even amid challenges. Gratitude practice helps children realize that no matter the struggle, there are always things to be thankful for. Some programs may do this in the form of prayer, meditation, or quiet reflection. It is important to note that children should never be forced to say something you are grateful for. It can take time for children to cultivate gratitude in a sincere and thoughtful way. It's best to let children share in their own time and listen to the examples of others who are ready to share their daily gratitude practice.

Mindfulness and Spirituality

Often these concepts have been viewed as separate or too personal to address in the realm of early childhood education, yet they are an undeniable

Tool use promotes perseverance as children try their hand at useful new skills.

CREDIT: HUMMINGBIRD HILL NATURE LEARNING COLLECTIVE, REISTERSTOWN, MARYLAND.

aspect of a child's holistic development. Historically there is a "perception in the western world that spirituality pertained to religious life and, therefore, was the prerogative of those belonging to a faith tradition. Such thinking firmly placed spirituality in the personal realm of individual and communal life" (de Souza 2016, 126). University of Maryland, Baltimore County (UMBC) professor Jennifer Mata-McMahon, in an attempt to understand how early childhood educators cultivate spirituality, defines spirituality as "An innate human characteristic, a potential we are all born with, which allows us to connect with something beyond us (transcendence or the divine), feel part of the greater universe, and be connected to otherness" (Mata-McMahon 2019, 53). She adds that spirituality is something that "encompasses the individual capacity and the essence of life, providing humans with a window to greater consciousness and more profound understanding of being, meaning, and purpose" (Mata-McMahon 2019, 53). This spiritual connection is essential to a sense of belonging and well-being that, in turn, empowers children to make positive contributions to a more socially cohesive learning community (de Souza 2016; Mata-McMahon 2019).

So how can spiritual growth be accomplished? One way is through a process of nurturing positive experiences of connectedness, which are abundant in nature-based education (de Souza 2016).

Group activities such as shelter-building are a great way for children to gain confidence in their abilities with the support of peers and teachers.

CREDIT: MONTESSORI LUNA BILINGUAL MICRO SCHOOL, PIKESVILLE, MARYLAND.

Not surprisingly, in Mata-McMahon's study, she found that educators cited natural settings such as the woods paired with child-directed play as catalysts to support spirituality (Mata-McMahon 2019). In fact, many studies refer back to E.O. Wilson's concept of biophilia (the innate tendency of humans to connect with other living things and nature discussed in Chapter 1's appendix) as the link that helps children feel a connection with other living things, which is key to nurturing spirituality (Schein 2014; Wilson 1984). Deborah Schein studies the intersection of nature and children's spirituality, and explains that "the concept of biophilia represented by a child's developing relationship with nature provides another deep connection ... and is required for stimulating and maintaining a child's spiritual development" (Schein 2014). Engagement with nature has repeatedly been found to enhance spiritual connection when children are given time to truly build a relationship with nature (Mata-McMahon 2019; Robinson 2019; Schein 2014).

A broad understanding of mindfulness, or a keen awareness, comes from heightened presence, curiosity, wonder, and awe that occur through encounters with the natural world. Indigenous groups have a range of traditional and cultural practices that ascribe land-based spirituality to a deep connection and relationship with nature. One study notes a "profound awareness, attunement, and reciprocity consistent with the broader definition of mindfulness" that comes from engagement with the land and supports learning and healing (Dylan & Smallboy 2016, 108; Walsh 2022). Through mindful activities that keep children focused on the present, such as a sensory outdoor "sit spot" (a place outside where one can sit quietly to observe nature and connect with their experience) and abundant time for children to explore nature through their play, children have time to be present and receptive to nature's wonder.

Emotional Well-Being and Stress Relief

Nature-based programs can provide a calm, relaxing environment that helps mitigate the effects of stress, which is a benefit experienced by both teachers and children (Louv 2005). Nature provides a restorative setting where children can pause and regroup without the pressure of focused tasks (Chawla & Nasar 2015). There is a growing body of research on the positive effects of urban green spaces on human well-being, which underscores the case for nature-based learning, no matter what the setting may be (Reyes-Riveros et al. 2021). Significantly, many of the values discussed here can lessen stress, anxiety, and other symptoms of mood disorders and mental health conditions. Nature-based programs provide safe ways to share and reflect on experiences, name emotions, and engage in conflict resolution with teachers who gently model the process. There are many opportunities for children to practice emotional regulation and consider the perspective of others, too.

In natural settings, "both natural daylight and physical activity relate to better mental health, and specifically to better affective and cognitive self-regulation" (Weeland et al. 2019, 2). Considering the increased activity through outdoor play in nature-based programs, these benefits are interrelated and have a dynamic positive effect. Furthermore, according to the Attention Restoration Theory (ART), "nature supports the replenishment of depleted resources, especially those related to cognitive self-regulation," which helps children attend to more structured academic tasks later in the day (Weeland et al. 2019, 2; Vella-Brodrick & Gilowska 2022). Specifically, the benefits of self-regulation from time spent in nature can be categorized into (1) promotive, (2) protective, and (3) restorative (Weeland et al. 2019). For these reasons, researchers urge schools to integrate "nature in the everyday experiences of young people to enhance mental health" (Vella-Brodrick & Gilowska 2022, 1246).

When children explore local habitats, they have opportunities to appreciate the plants and animals that reside there.

CREDIT: ASSOCIATION FOR NATURE-BASED EDUCATION, NOTCHCLIFF NATURE PROGRAMS.

Nature Connection and Environmental Literacy

Children develop a sense of belonging and interconnectedness through nature play. This fundamental understanding helps children form ecological identity as an important part of the greater natural world (this will be discussed in further detail in Chapter 3). A heightened awareness and connection to nature sets the tone for lifelong stewardship, caretaking, and action on behalf of nature and vital natural resources.

Cognitive and Intellectual Development

Intellectual development refers to changes in the brain that help us think and process information. It involves complex genetic, social, and environmental factors, which make it challenging to consider this aspect of early development in isolation. Helpful examples of intellectual (also referred to as "cognitive") skills include reasoning, making judgments, executive functioning, problem solving, language use, innovation, imagination, reflection, and many forms of inquiry. These skills help us make sense of the world and are especially critical in the formative years because up to 90 percent of a child's brain development occurs before age 6.

Recent findings show that a child's intellectual development is significantly enhanced through nature-based learning and play (Vovides & Lemus 2019). Studies show that children reap benefits of playful nature-based programs and that the benefits outlast the short-term gains that are made in more academic settings (memorized sight words, for example). Children demonstrate significant gains in STEM-based learning in rural, suburban, and urban schools when nature-based learning and play are incorporated into the curriculum (Sprague et al. 2020).

One explanation for these gains may have to do with the Zone of Proximal Development (ZPD) (Vygotsky 1978). Psychologist Lev Vygotsky describes ZPD as a set of optimal learning conditions, or a sweet spot, where children can learn something new. This happens when a child is faced with a challenge that is motivating yet difficult, one not too easy to accomplish or downright unachievable. Vygotsky explains that the ZPD is "the distance between the action development level as determined by independent problem solving and the level of potential development as determined through problem solving under adult guidance or in collaboration with more capable peers" (Vygotsky 1978, 86). In nature-based education, children operate within their ZPD on a highly individualized basis as children freely choose their learning, and teachers scaffold further learning opportunities to fuel their interests.

Executive Functioning Skills

Nature-based learning and play involves a range of executive functioning skills, including problem solving, conscious self-regulation and inhibition control, and the use of working memory. Nature

Loose-parts play can include some surprising little friends, like this worm!

CREDIT: FALLS CHURCH–MCLEAN CHILDREN'S CENTER.

play requires children to use open-ended natural materials that presents opportunities to practice divergent thinking and reasoning skills. For example, children may want to build a shelter with leaves and branches and realize that not all branches are large or sturdy, so they have to problem-solve—they may choose a bigger log to support smaller branches or use grass to tie sticks together.

In a recent study, researchers found that "nature-based practices were more effective in supporting hot executive control (HEC) and attention/impulse control than programs with less incorporation of nature-based practices" (Ernst & Stelley 2024, 14). These two terms—hot executive control and attention/impulse control—help describe differences in executive functioning skills. Hot executive control refers to "scenarios such as not taking a toy that belongs to another child, not becoming angry when a task becomes too challenging, and the ability to delay gratification" (Ernst

& Stelley 2024, 8). In comparison, cool executive control refers to a range of "organized, flexible, goal-directed cognitive processes in response to non-affective (non-emotional) stimuli" (Ernst & Stelley 2024, 7). The findings of this study point to "potential for greater equity in terms of who experiences and ultimately benefits from nature by extending the use of nature-based practices beyond the private into public preschool settings" (Ernst & Stelley 2024, 14).

Blossoming Imagination

Children take inspiration from their surroundings. They become more resourceful, creative, and innovative when learning takes place in a natural learning environment with natural materials. Chawla and Nasar (2015) note that "natural areas provide for more imaginative, constructive, sensory, and socially cooperative play than asphalt, flat expanses of lawn, or built play equipment" (445). There is a bit of mystery and magic to the inner workings of nature, especially to young children. When an autumn wind blows and colorful leaves rain from the sky, a beautiful, palpable sense of wonder also fills the air. When children come upon a tuft of fur or cluster of feathers on the ground, they begin to make predictions to try and make sense of what happened. This often spills into their imaginative play.

Additional research underscores the possibilities of nature-based materials, both inside and outside of the classroom (Chookah et al. 2024; Vella-Brodrick & Gilowska 2022; Vovides & Lemus 2019). Because nature-based programs prioritize natural materials and settings, they are highly selective about toys or commercialized playthings in the learning environment. This invites children to bring their own ideas to the materials they interact with. For example, children may fasten a large sycamore leaf to a stick to make a puppet or repurpose a cardboard box to be a fox den during pretend play. Make-believe worlds unfold with the incorporation of natural and recycled loose parts when they are made available to children (Cankaya et al. 2023).

As previously discussed, nature-based education prioritizes child-directed play when children are viewed as capable of independent decision-making and leaves space for children to freely make choices and explore their ideas, which promotes creative thinking and problem solving. Hunter-Doniger (2021) notes that "creativity, autonomy, and play (CAP) were constants in the child-centered approaches and rarely occurred in isolation because there were continuously seamless interconnections taking place" (24). Nature-based education, thanks to its emphasis on child-directed learning, also supports creativity in this way.

Reduced Effects of Attention Deficit Hyperactivity Disorder

Attention deficit hyperactivity disorder (ADHD) is defined as a "neurodevelopmental disorder with childhood onset and core symptoms of inattention, hyperactivity, and impulsivity, which often persist into adolescence and adulthood" (Thygesen et al. 2020, 127011-4). Because there is a range of symptoms and manifestations, this condition has also been referred to as ADD, or attention deficit disorder. Numerous studies find that children experience diminished symptoms of ADHD when provided with greater access to nature (Taylor et al. 2001; Thygesen et al. 2020). Benefits include better concentration, less inattention, and reduced impulsivity. Taylor and colleagues (2001) examined the power of the ART and its implications on children with ADHD. They explain that people rely on two kinds of attention (Kaplan 1995). The first is directed attention that is needed for focused tasks such as writing a note or following a recipe. The second is involuntary attention, which is relatively easier for our brains, as we notice things like a squirrel rustling in leaves or a scent wafting on a breeze. Their research proposes that natural environments assist directed attention (Kaplan 1995; Taylor et al. 2001). In a more recent study, findings show that regular exposure to green spaces directly results in reduced severity of symptoms for ADHD (Taylor & Kuo 2011). This was true regardless of gender or socio-economic factors. Their evidence highlights that "children with ADHD who play regularly in green play settings have milder symptoms than children who play in built outdoor and indoor settings" (Taylor & Kuo 2011, 296). Furthermore, "when the directed attentional system is fatigued, providing an opportunity to deploy the less effortful fascination system can allow the directed attentional system time to recover" (Schutte et al. 2017, 5). Interestingly, "studies have found that children with ADHD have lower gut microbial diversity and that increased microbial exposure from the environment can improve the microbial diversity," which may also reduce the symptoms of ADHD (Thygesen et al. 2020, 127011-2). Given the task-oriented focus in many traditional school settings, immersion in natural and green settings is a welcome reprieve that benefits children with ADHD.

Greater Engagement

Nature-based learning provides hands-on experience that is engaging and highly motivating for young children. When children's level of engagement increases, so does their enthusiasm toward content-driven activities in areas such as science, history, and math. This opens opportunities for interdisciplinary learning across content areas by integrating natural materials, artifacts, and outdoor settings as part of the curriculum. For example, if teachers want children to learn about the life cycle of a frog, a classroom-based teacher may provide a worksheet to color that shows eggs, tadpoles, froglets, and frogs. Perhaps students may cut out the pictures to make a mobile or art project. Compare that with children who go for a nature walk to listen for frogs, identify a good habitat for frogs, and investigate a stream or pond in search of frog eggs and tadpoles. The sensory engagement and interaction is dynamic and rich in comparison, which makes the experience more memorable. As a result, they are more likely to develop an understanding of the life cycle of a frog. Indeed, they may also discover related plants and animals that are part of a local aquatic habitat. Cudworth and Tymms examine how nature-based learning is beneficial. They reiterate that "pressure on schools to focus their time on performativity has cemented the idea that all learning takes place inside the school, is curriculum and teacher-led and determined by classroom practices alone," which has "led to an overall decline in many schools of the pedagogical value of experiential outdoor activities and play-based learning" (Cudworth & Tymms 2023, 491). By contrast, nature-based learning is largely child directed, thereby providing a higher level of engagement. In addition, because nature-based learning often takes place in natural outdoor settings, there are "opportunities for children to experience activities in smaller groups, encouraging social interaction rather than passive learning" (Richardson & Murray 2017, 466). This high level of engagement stands to benefit learners across content and developmental domains.

Language Development

Nature-based programs have effective yet natural approaches to language development. Children are exposed to and immersed in a wide range of experiences that foster expressive and receptive language, reading, and writing skills (Richardson et al. 2024). In a study of children involved in a forest school program, their "clarity of speech is shown to have improved, and range of vocabulary and listening and attention skills have improved" (Richardson 2014, 11). At the same time, they found "the most significant impact is that on social communication" (Richardson 2014, 11). Further studies have revealed that "within the natural environment, where learning is child-initiated, the quality of utterances manifest in ways not found in indoor or outdoor classrooms, where learning is adult led" (Richardson & Murray 2017, 457). In fact, the same study finds the application of language variations is increased in outdoor settings, which includes increased usage of verbs (learning is active!) and adjectives (learning is sensory!) as well as exclamation usage (learning is fun!), all of which indicate "positive links between the natural environment and children's expressive language" (Richardson & Murray 2017, 466).

The following examples highlight language development in nature-based programs.

Storytelling

Whether children retell a trail adventure, spin a creative new tale, dictate elements of a story, offer group reflection as "stories of the day," or listen to someone else's story, children make meaning through the culture of oral storytelling. Sharing stories as a group helps build descriptive vocabulary, develops confidence in public speaking, and hones comprehension skills. At the same time, storytelling establishes a supportive atmosphere where people listen respectfully and all are welcome to share ideas. Storytelling offers a playful way to retell the sequence of the day's activities—for example, relaying the discoveries made during a trail walk or reflecting on important emergent learning. This can reinforce the connections children make with elements of nature independently and establish a shared understanding of learning as a class community. Story stones, mystery nature treasures, and a talking stick are examples of activities that promote storytelling.

Direct experiences are an engaging way to cultivate empathy for living things, like this monarch caterpillar.

CREDIT: LIVE & LEARN EARLY LEARNING CENTER, LEE, NEW HAMPSHIRE..

Chalk is a useful material to encourage marking with something nontoxic and temporary in outdoor settings.

CREDIT: LIVE & LEARN EARLY LEARNING CENTER, LEE, NEW HAMPSHIRE.

Maps

Children can apply place-based knowledge about the land by drawing and reading maps. Mapmaking provides opportunities for children to develop spatial awareness as they deepen their sense of place. Creating a map is a complex process that requires decisions around "what to show, how to show it and what not to show, and for what reasons" (Kvernbekk & Jarning 2019, 560). Maps also use symbols to "deconstruct a part of the world and then reassemble it" (Kvernbekk & Jarning 2019, 560). Often created as a class, maps help children explore how symbols represent places they visit. Spatial awareness, learning landmarks, and place names are all benefits of making and using maps. Children also deepen their connection to places when they make maps. For ideas, see David Sobel's book *Mapmaking with Children: Sense-of-Place Education for the Elementary Years* (1998).

Field Guides

It used to be that our ancestors were the keepers of knowledge about the plants and animals around us, and they would hand down this knowledge through generations as part of community life and experience. Today, we have volumes of information in the form of printed and digital resources. While the collection of information in field guides is incredible, the paired experience of learning and applying new information is still key. In nature-based programs, children observe and compare features of plants, animals, rocks, nests, and tracks with images found in field guides. This helps children discriminate identifying traits while learning about characteristics such as size, color, shape, markings, and quantity of petals or leaflets. Field guides encourage children to read for a purpose and can also be useful online and as apps. Both visual and audio field guides are useful, such as iNaturalist or the Merlin bird app by Cornell Lab. An extension of using field guides is that children are empowered to create localized, site-specific field guides with digital photos, drawings, and labels to indicate special features, which deepens place-based connections as well.

Nature journals like the one seen here often include seasonal materials such as dandelions.

CREDIT: MONTESSORI LUNA BILINGUAL MICRO SCHOOL, PIKESVILLE, MARYLAND.

Nature Journals

The blank pages in a nature journal or sketchbook can provide an array of opportunities for children to express what they experience in nature. The following activities nurture reading and writing skills through all sorts of experiments with natural materials:

› Drawing and mark-making: Free-form drawing may explore a natural material (e.g., stick dipped in mud), approximate something from life (e.g., bird on a branch), document something from the past, imagine a new idea/story, or experiment with the sensation and control of using novel materials on a piece of paper. Drawing may be done with traditional drawing materials such as pencils or markers or may be created with plentiful natural materials.

- Rubbings: Textured impressions from leaves, flowers, feathers, bark, shells, and similar items.

- Tracing: Careful outlines of natural objects to replicate their size and shape.

- Smooshing: Pressing or squeezing items to see what color and consistency might appear from a natural material such as a flower head, berry, or seedpod.

- Smashing: Breaking apart a natural material to see what is inside and whether or not it could make a mark, such as a clump of soil, rock, or fruit rind.

- Collage: Gluing or taping natural or recycled materials in a pleasing arrangement or pattern.

- Sewing: Stitching through paper with grasses, twine, or vine, for example, or sewing pockets into the journal for collections.

- Paints and dyes: Natural materials that have been combined with water (or, in some cases, boiled to extract pigment) to create paint or dye, or experiment with watercolors or tempera paint to create images.

- Printmaking: Using natural materials with ink or a thin layer of paint to make a print such as leaves, ferns, or mushroom gills, or create stamps or printing plates that can make many prints.

- Weaving: By first adding threads to create a weft, children can weave natural materials onto journal pages.

- Photographs: May be used in conjunction with collage either with photos from class

This nature journal features flower petals and flower heads along with a child's written descriptions.

CREDIT: MONTESSORI LUNA BILINGUAL MICRO SCHOOL, PIKESVILLE, MARYLAND.

The simplicity of writing letters on leaves creates possibilities for spelling.

CREDIT: HUMMINGBIRD HILL NATURE LEARNING COLLECTIVE, REISTERSTOWN, MARYLAND.

> or from nature magazines; photos may be glued into journal and then labeled to document a special experience, observation, or idea.

> › Labeling: Child writes or dictates the names for various elements in their journal imagery; these may be precise labels for plants and animals they have drawn, or they may be inventive names.

> › Dictating/Documentation: An extension of journaling, teacher prompts child to "tell me about this picture" and then records verbatim what the child dictates along with date; these may be matter-of-fact statements about their work, elaborate stories, or vivid recollections.

Names and Signs

Children develop a strong sense of place when they come to know elements of the natural world and bestow their own special names on things. Naming allows children to experiment with descriptive language around a shared experience of place. (This is a great tie-in to storytelling, mapmaking, and nature journals, too.) Children may stop to read signs along the trail, near the school, or at the park. Signage also presents opportunities to point out words and place names, recognize letters, and make letter sounds. Child-made wayfinding signs and labels are another way to incorporate writing, and they encourage a greater sense of belonging and connection to place. For example, "the Magic River" may be a special name given by children to note an important body of water. They can build on their language skills as they draw, write, tell stories, and make signs about it.

Music and Song

Sounds collide with harmonious or rhythmic spoken words as children learn about elements of nature through song. They may invent songs, create new verses to familiar songs, or simply clap along while others sing or sign. Children can learn to recognize melodic sounds in nature such as the trill of a chorus frog or nasally call of a chickadee with phonetic sounds that they can repeat. The tapping of a woodpecker, whoosh of autumn trees overhead in wind, or the trickle of a brook can all be connected to aspects of musicality. There are many songs and fingerplays that are inspired by nature, which can promote understanding about animals and help children discover rhyming words.

> ### "My Paddle's Keen and Bright" by Margaret Embers McGee (1918)
> My paddle's keen and bright
>
> Flashing with silver
>
> Follow the wild goose flight
>
> Dip, dip, and swing. Dip, dip, and swing.

While singing this song, children can pretend to dip a paddle back and forth in the water as they sing.

Children may also be inspired to create instruments that mimic sounds in nature or utilize natural materials to create music. Clay bird whistles, rattles made from gourds, and wooden flutes are a few that come to mind. As children develop a repertoire of nature-based songs, they have opportunities for musical expression and appreciation. Campfires and circle gathering experiences are both wonderful examples of how vocal and instrumental songs may be shared in community.

> **Songlines**
>
> A fascinating intersection of song and place comes in the form of "songlines," which is part of many Indigenous traditions that draw deep connections to the land. In Australia, for example, songlines carry "information about the land, encoding the locations of resources across the landscape throughout the seasons, and mapping sacred spaces and notable places" (Higgins 2021, 723). In North America, at least 142 known tribal "Salt Songs" crisscross from the Pacific Ocean to the Grand Canyon (Engelhard 2016). As with other songlines, "trails codified by these songs align sacred and historical sites, ancient villages, hunting or burial grounds, and places for the gathering of medicinal herbs—and salt, a valued commodity" (Engelhard 2016, 7). There are many accounts of the ways Indigenous Peoples use songlines for wayfinding and connection to the land and, in many cases, a deep spiritual connection to their history and culture. "More than just musical travelogue or mnemonic device, the song cycle roots a people in place" (Engelhard 2016, 18). When children are encouraged to think of song in this way, it can stitch songs deeply into a child's connection to the local landscape and the special places therein.

Dramatic Play

Dramatic play (or pretend play) allows children to socialize, apply language skills, and explore themes from real life or their imaginations. Children often use natural materials as part of their dramatic-play scenarios. Because nature-based programs provide generous amounts of time for children to engage in unstructured nature play (which is akin to free play with the benefit of being in nature), this is an ideal time for dramatic play to emerge: "Researchers argue that free play; activity that is spontaneous and directed by the child, supports children's optimum involvement in dramatic play" (Robertson et al. 2020, 378). Dramatic play is positively linked to executive functioning skills as well. A recent study finds that "social pretend play is predictive of gains in inhibitory control more than solitary pretend and social non-pretend play" (Ernst & Stelley 2024, 3).

Capes, tails, and headbands can all help children "become" animals in their dramatic play.

CREDIT: HUMMINGBIRD HILL NATURE LEARNING COLLECTIVE, REISTERSTOWN, MARYLAND.

Questioning

A natural outgrowth of the process of inquiry is asking questions! Too often, adults are quick to answer a child's question, instead of encouraging the child to engage in further inquiry and discover the answer on their own. Keep the "quest" in questions by resisting the urge to give answers. Instead, ask follow-up questions that help lead a child to find their own answers. Nature-based programs invite children to follow their interests, which involves asking (and often answering) many questions. Curiosity dovetails into inquiry-based learning and can be the motivation to examine all kinds of mysterious questions about nature! Asking questions is an integral part of a young child's learning and serves an important purpose: "Children's inquisitiveness is not just random, it is strategic" (Wong et al. 2024, 17). The act of questioning is another way to apply language and comprehension skills to make meaning of the world. Nature-based learning is full of wonder and inspires many questions, which often require ongoing observations to answer.

Encounters with Animals and Other Surprises in Nature

Early childhood is an important time to instill positive attitudes about animals and nature. Feelings of empathy are increased with direct contact and exposure to nature, including animals that may not be considered "cute," such as worms or spiders (Kos et al. 2023). Researchers in a recent study note that "A positive attitude towards nature should be intrinsic to the entire teaching staff dealing with children during their preschool and school period, and with student teachers during their professional development" to help instill such positive attitudes towards the natural world (Kos et al. 2023, 94–95). Nature is full of surprises that provide opportunities for hands-on discovery as children expand their vocabulary around plants, animals, weather, natural processes, and life cycles. As children encounter new ideas, they also learn verbs that describe the activity around them. Position words are used generously as they describe where things are and how they are moving outdoors. Repetition of animal calls and sounds can support phonemic awareness and exploration of sounds used in speech. Tactile experiences can reinforce learning about letters and their sounds, such as slithering like a snake through tall grass ("Ss"), tracing "Mm" in mud or moss, wrapping willow branches into wreaths ("Ww"), or leaping into a large pile of leaves ("Ll").

Chapter 2

These direct experiences help cultivate a sense of wonder that is inextricably linked to human-nature connection. According to Joergensen (2016), "Local practices of being outdoors in nature and on wild places has an intrinsic value for the children allowing them to develop their own play" (1154). Not surprisingly, "It is also a way to get firsthand experiences from the nature we live in" (Joergensen 2016, 1154).

Games

Children negotiate their ideas, reject or play by agreed rules, and develop the structure of games of their own design when given ample time for unstructured outdoor nature play. Inventing games involves reflection, processing others' ideas, developing strategy, turn taking, and discussion with others to play cooperatively. Researchers studying games in natural outdoor settings explain: "Games involve risks, which have the function of bringing children closer to stimuli capable of awakening an innate fear (heights, speed, loud noises) and which support the progressive development of strategies to cope with such situations" (García-González & Schenetti 2022, 366). When children play outdoor games, they must remember rules of the game and at the same time make choices about their play amid interaction with others. This means that many language skills are involved in children's games, too. The games may be predetermined, such as tic-tac-toe or hopscotch, or they may be invented as part of children's play. Summarized neatly: "In a society which offers ready access to virtual reality, the relationship with the natural environment should take on more weight and value, especially in children's lives, and adults should reflect seriously on the quality of the experiences that children are living and that teachers are offering in schools" (García-González & Schenetti 2022, 366–367).

Children scoop up water and mud as they examine what lives in the pond.

Outdoor story time can reinforce new ideas about nature such as the changing weather, seasons, plants, and animals.

CREDIT: FALLS CHURCH–MCLEAN CHILDREN'S CENTER.

Children's Books and Poetry

Printed literature is rich with illustrations, stories, and meaningful concepts for children to explore about nature-based topics. By providing a rotating assortment of seasonal books, magazines, poetry, and field guides, children have access to print materials for independent and small-group reading. A curated selection of books is provided here to accommodate children who speak multiple languages and to ensure that different kinds of families, cultures, and abilities are represented. In immersive outdoor programs, teachers often laminate full picture books and attach pages with binder rings so children can also have books available, even in wet weather.

Favorite Children's Stories & Field Guides

A Walk in the Forest by Maria Dek

An Egg Is Quiet by Dianna Aston

Berry Song by Michaela Goade

Birdhouse for Rent by Harriet Ziefert

Bird Watch Book for Kids: Introduction to Birdwatching, Colorful Guide to 25 Popular Backyard Birds, and Journal Pages by Dylanna Press

Goodbye Autumn, Hello Winter by Kenard Pak

Home: Where Our Story Begins by Britta Teckentrup

Leaf Man by Lois Ehlert

Little Cloud by Eric Carle

The Hike by Alison Farrell

The Honeybee by Kirsten Hall

The Magic & Mystery of Trees by Jen Green

The Other Way to Listen by Byrd Baylor

The Shortest Day by Susan Cooper

Hello, World! Rocks and Minerals by Jill McDonald

How Plants Talk by Helena Haraštová

Humongous Fungus by Lynne Boddy

Lola Plants a Garden by Anna McQuinn

Me and My Sit Spot by Lauren MacLean

Not a Stick by Antoinette Portis

One Little Bug: Exploring Nature for Curious Kids by Becky Davies

Our Planet! There's No Place Like Earth by Stacy McAnulty

Outside In by Deborah Underwood

Snowflake Bentley by Jacqueline Briggs Martin

Thank You, Earth: A Love Letter to Our Planet: A Springtime Book for Kids by April Pulley Sayre

Tiny, Perfect Things by M.H. Clark

Tracks, Scats and Signs by Leslie Dendy

Up in the Garden and Down in the Dirt by Kate Messner

We All Play by Julie Flett

We Are All Connected: Caring for Each Other & the Earth by Gabi Garcia

Wonder Walkers by Micha Archer

Worm Weather by Jean Taft

Cooking

Because nature-based programs grow a strong sense of place, tasting and cooking are usually a component of outdoor learning. Experiences include learning to identify edible and medicinal plants in the immediate area; foraging and harvesting foods; growing herbs, fruits, and vegetables; and learning to cook with them in community. As with other nature-based activities, there are wonderful opportunities for children to learn new vocabulary, listen and express ideas, and write, draw, or map ideas about the foods they taste. Children often write down recipes and invent new ones, which can play out in elaborate scenarios in a "mud kitchen." The term "mud kitchen" is used to describe a designated space where children use cooking and baking items such as pots, pans, rolling pins, whisks, baking sheets, and mortar and pestles for pretend play and combine them with seasonal loose parts from nature such as pine needles, berries, sand, flowers, stones, twigs, seedpods, and, yes, soil. When combined with (rain) water—you guessed it—children can also make mud. These spaces spark rich, imaginative social play. Cookbooks and recipe cards are a great addition to a mud kitchen space.

Often children and families share foods that are part of their cultural traditions. Families may be invited to share special recipes, gather during local harvest times, or cook together during campfire events. For example, roasted chestnuts or squash may be cooked over a fire to welcome the winter solstice, or children may gather dandelions and make fritters to welcome spring. Cooking activities provide opportunities to hone connection to the natural world as well as to read, write, and taste recipes, and to learn more about one another.

Local History

Children discover important aspects of the land, local Indigenous groups, early settlements, notable historical events, and other traditions in the community through an ongoing combination of reading, oral storytelling, plays, and poetry. School-age children may get involved in research about local lore, meet local figures or tribal representatives, or read accounts from historical societies. Sharing written accounts or historical photos of the grounds and people who lived there can inspire wonderful learning about the history of the land. For example, when children unearthed an old horseshoe and glass jar at their forest school, it led them to deeper inquiry about the horse farm and orchard that were once part of the property. (This also shares links with storytelling, mapmaking, music, naming, games, and cooking.)

These examples offer a glimpse into some of the many direct experiences that are beneficial for children to develop language in nature-based programs.

Children have a mushy yet satisfying "cooking" experience in the mud kitchen.

CREDIT: BLUESTONE VILLAGE AND NATURE PROGRAMS.

Dandelion Fritter Recipe *From* Justin Pegnataro

1. Collect the dandelion flower heads, as many as you like, and then rinse them.
2. Dip the flower heads in eggs that have already been beaten. You may want to dust the flower heads with flour first to help get the egg to stick, but it's not necessary.
3. Dip the flower heads in breadcrumbs that have been mixed with salt and pepper.
4. Gently fry in olive oil, using a fork or tongs to turn them. Cook them until they are golden brown and crispy.
5. Drain on a paper towel, and then they are ready to eat!

Understanding Skills, Content, and Values Through Nature Play

Given all of the benefits of nature-based learning, educators may wonder how to facilitate experiences for their students in a way that seamlessly blends early learning standards. Because early learning standards vary widely from state to state, Table 2.1 lists developmental domains with a skill or value that may be part of a typical early childhood curriculum. The right-hand column provides examples that demonstrate how learning might unfold in a nature-based program.

It is astounding to consider all the ways that nature-based education prepares a foundation for future learning through hands-on experiences! Although these are but a few examples, Table 2.1 illustrates how nature-based learning is an engaging, holistic approach that enhances learning across developmental domains.

The more time children spend in nature, the more benefits they will experience from it. Here a child examines a tree during the Forest Days Outdoor Learning Program, hosted by ANBE in Philadelphia, Pennsylvania, over the last five years.

CREDIT: ASSOCIATION FOR NATURE-BASED EDUCATION, FOREST DAYS OUTDOOR LEARNING PROGRAM.

Table 2.1 Developmental Domains, Skills, and Values

Developmental Domain*	Skills and Values	Example
Physical Development/ Physical Education and Health	Fine motor skills: Sensory integration	Child picks up pine needles, acorns, and maple seeds
	Gross motor skills: Vestibular sense	Child uses their balance to walk across a wobbly log
	Locomotor skills and proprioception	Child gallops down a hill, pretending to be a deer
	Gross motor skills: Proprioception	Child rolls down a hill
	Identify ways that people and objects move (physical education)	Child observes peers maneuvering a wagon and then attempts to pull the wagon on their own
	Identify ways to care for your body (health)	Child eats a cherry tomato grown in the school's outside garden
	Demonstrate safety in physically active settings (health)	Child carries long branch upright, dragging one end on the ground
	Identify ways to care for your body (health)	Child puts on own hat and mittens on a cold day
Social Foundations/ Social-Emotional Development	Perspective-taking	Child imagines how a snail might feel and makes a choice based on another creature's perspective
	Describe emotions	Child describes frustration when putting on their backpack
	Initiate and maintain relationships with peers	Child holds up a special leaf and invites another child to see it
	Regulate emotions and manage expectations	Child is thrilled to discover a toad yet learns how to watch patiently to avoid scaring it away
	Attentiveness: Resists distraction to maintain focus on tasks of interest to the child	Child steadily works on making a "fairy forest" using twigs and other loose parts while others play group games nearby
	Demonstrate flexibility and adapt to consider others' needs	Child wants to keep digging with a shovel but recognizes another child has been waiting for a turn

Chapter 2

49

Table 2.1 (*Continued*)

Developmental Domain*	Skills and Values	Example
Cognitive/ Intellectual Development (This domain contains subject areas such as math, science, social studies, engineering, fine arts, and technology.)	Measure with nonstandard units (math)	Child uses a length of twine to measure and compare the diameter of trees
	Describe and compare measurable attributes (math)	Child picks up two stones and uses a scale to note the different weight of each
	Identify patterns in real-life situations (math)	Child observes pattern of opposite branching (side branches, buds, and leaves grow directly across from each other on the stem) in maple trees
	Identify and describe two-dimensional shapes (math)	Children name the shapes of leaves (circle, oval, star) and backpack items (field guide is a rectangle, bandana is a square)
	Observation and inquiry (science)	Child notices which birds eat seeds from a bird feeder and which birds eat seeds on the ground
	Use tools to extend senses and gather data (science)	Child uses magnifying glass to get a closer look at an ant
	Distinguish among past, present, and future time (social studies)	Child observes changes in a compost bin as food scraps decay to soil over time
	Describe how the community has changed over time and how people have contributed to its change, drawing from maps, photographs, news, and other sources (social studies)	Children discover old stone wall that historically divided property on the grounds and compare it to photos from local historical society
	Show that a problem might have multiple solutions or no solution (engineering)	Child makes a garland of leaves but must experiment to determine which leaves are sturdy and which tear easily
	Develop the ability to recognize music as a form of individual and cultural expression through experiencing music as both personal and societal expression (fine arts: music)	Child sings goodbye song at the end of class and inserts their own verse to the song to personalize it
	Describe processes used to interpret and express ideas in the visual arts and other disciplines (fine arts: visual)	Children use animal track stamps to create a mural about local animals

(*Continued*)

Table 2.1 (*Continued*)

Developmental Domain*	Skills and Values	Example
	Use a variety of theatrical elements to communicate ideas and feelings (fine arts: theater)	Child uses a stick as a magic wand and performs "spells" on peers who join in the performance
	Develop ability to improvise dance (fine arts: dance)	Child moves their body like a seed floating on the wind
Language and Literacy Development	Receptive language	Child listens to peer reflections about the day
	Expressive language	Child tells a peer about the fluffy seeds bursting from a milkweed pod
	Acquire new vocabulary	Child discovers an unusual creature that leads to learning new vocabulary about millipedes and centipedes
	Sequencing events	Child retells experiences in the order that they happened along a trail walk
	Dictate, draw, or write to inform	Child draws a picture of a woodpecker in nature journal and indicates traits of the bird's beak and feet
	Participate in collaborative conversations with diverse partners about topics and texts with peers and adults in small and larger groups	Child offers a guess during circle gathering about a tuft of fur that was found on a tree
Spiritual Development	Develop a personal relationship with nature; develop a personal understanding and connection to something that is larger than oneself	Child considers how to honor a dead bird and suggests burying it and decorating its resting place
Environmental Literacy**	Participate in a variety of social interactions, including play and exploration in the outdoors, to grow as contributing members of their community	Child plants and waters seedlings with peers to create native flower gardens for pollinators
	Develop curiosity, ask their own questions, and begin to develop reasoning and problem-solving skills	Child discovers a hole in the ground and begins to observe clues in the vicinity to learn more about how it may have gotten there and who lives there
	Develop knowledge related to environmental and social systems, including the place where they live	Child learns to identify and responsibly harvest wild onion grass

Developmental Domain*	Skills and Values	Example
	Develop ability to investigate, analyze, and respond to environmental changes, situations, and concerns	Child notices how patches of ice have recently formed and explores safe ways to navigate them with support from teachers
	Experience a variety of environmental conditions	Child goes outdoors during every season in all kinds of weather, including rain, sun, and snow
	Develop empathy and increased self-reliance; demonstrate a sense of personal responsibility toward others and their environment; teachers model environmentally responsible actions and provide opportunities for children to make decisions about their own activities	Child zips their own coat and carries their own backpack, then offers to help a friend with their gear

*Many of the skills listed alongside developmental domains are based on Maryland Early Learning Standards (Maryland State Department of Education 2024).

**Environmental literacy skills are based on guidelines 4.1–4.5 in *Early Childhood Environmental Education Programs: Guidelines for Excellence* (NAAEE 2010).

Can Everyone Access These Benefits?

All children have a right to access the benefits of nature-based early childhood education. But questions of equitable access and environmental justice permeate nearly every aspect of this discussion. For example, barriers may exist to safely explore the outdoors, including:

› Harmful air pollutants such as smoke or smog
› Hazardous litter such as broken glass or drug paraphernalia
› Hazardous contaminants in the soil, groundwater, or streams
› Frequent crime or violence in the vicinity
› Inaccessibility to outdoor sites for children with disabilities
› Potentially dangerous wildlife (e.g., stray dogs, venomous snakes, or mountain lions)
› Lack of gear to allow children to go outdoors safely in cold weather
› Busy street, parking lot, or traffic nearby

Layered approaches are needed to tackle some of the toughest challenges of poverty, crime, and pollution. That said, there are steps programs and educators can take to counteract some of these challenges. Exposure to nature provides stress reduction, so for children enmeshed in stressful learning environments, "exposure to nature can help children to replenish depleted cognitive resources resulting from information overload. An attraction to nature can trigger 'soft' (effortless) fascination, relieve fatigue and aid psychological replenishing" (Vella-Brodrick & Gilowska 2022, 1219). Chapter 4 provides suggestions for working with families and the community to make nature-based learning safe and available to all children.

Consider the many ways that nature-based learning supports healthy, holistic child development and overall well-being. As you think about your work with young children, consider which nature-based activities and experiences may be ideal in your early learning environment.

CALL TO ACTION

Introduce the use of nature journals to support language and literacy skills. Nature journals may be created by the students or purchased as unlined sketchbooks. Brainstorm at least five nature-based activities that incorporate language and literacy skills and align with your curriculum, then try them in nature journals. If you already use nature journals, think of five new or modified ways to use them. As an educator, create your own nature journal and begin a practice of making observations in the natural world to model journaling with children.

NOTE: Clare Walker Leslie and Charles E. Roth have written a wonderful resource that may help spark ideas, *Keeping a Nature Journal* (2021).

Reflection Questions

> Why should schools embrace nature-based practices?
> What are the most surprising benefits of nature-based learning?
> Consider the skills and values that your current curriculum places emphasis on. List three nature-based approaches that may enhance learner engagement in these areas.

CHAPTER 3

Nature-Based Learning and Play

It can be challenging to define "education" without "play" because they are inseparably linked—or at least they should be—in early childhood education. Too often, early learning programs are so focused on standards that the programs become overly academic and structured, which can leave little time for play. In some cases, teachers may view play as what happens if there is time after the "real" learning is finished. This happens despite decades of research that tells us play is how young children learn best! In the book *All Work and No Play … How Educational Reforms Are Harming Our Preschoolers*, Joan Almon describes the importance of children's play, stating, "They continually develop new skills and capacities, and if they are allowed to set the pace with a bit of help from the adult world, they will work at all this in a playful and tireless way" (Almon 2003, 85). The reality is that child-directed play is what affords the most meaningful opportunities for learning. The process of education does not present us with an either/or situation (i.e., either children play outdoors *or* learn academic content). For young children, learning is play and play is learning. This chapter examines play-based learning within the context of nature play.

Guiding Questions

As you read through this chapter, consider the following questions:

- Does your curriculum allow for child-directed nature play? How does teacher-guided learning support unstructured play-based learning?

- To what extent do you incorporate unstructured nature play each day? Compare your approaches used for indoor and outdoor learning environments.

Play-Based Learning in Nature-Based Early Childhood Education

Nature-based educators have the pleasure of facilitating play-based learning within the context of nature pedagogy and the environment in which they teach. Nature play provides many ways for educators to introduce content and stimulate skill development based on what the season and the natural environment offer on any given day. The interplay between teachers, children, the environment, and all the experiences in between is where the seemingly magic learning takes place. It is up to teachers, in unison with program administrators, to prioritize the right balance of these experiences to support curricular goals.

Nature-based education emphasizes child-directed learning and play, including unstructured nature play. As described in the "7 Principles of Nature-Based Early Childhood Education" in the Introduction, teachers are facilitators who guide meaningful learning opportunities, manage risk, and provide individualized accommodations to support every child's needs. Importantly, as teachers facilitate play, they can support early learning goals by scaffolding concepts and skills found in the curriculum.

Teacher-Guided Versus Teacher-Directed

It is important to understand the differences between *teacher-guided* learning and *teacher-directed* learning. Teacher-guided approaches allow for open-ended, unstructured play. Teacher-guided approaches are based on observation of children's interests and prior knowledge, which allows teachers to scaffold new learning based on ideas and interests sparked by children.

In contrast, teacher-directed learning, sometimes called direct instruction, is used to introduce targeted knowledge, skills, vocabulary, or concepts to children in a specific way. Teacher-directed learning features an objective or set of objectives that the teacher aims to meet, which can be helpful to examine one skill or topic in isolation but can also prevent emergent learning opportunities if the teacher's focus is solely on the preplanned objective(s). In some cases, teacher-directed instruction is unrelated

Bonds of friendship and other social-emotional development naturally unfold during nature play.

CREDIT: LIVE & LEARN EARLY LEARNING CENTER, LEE, NEW HAMPSHIRE.

Children combine sand play with other nature elements in the outdoor environment.

CREDIT: GOOSEBERRY NATURE SCHOOL, COVINGTON, KENTUCKY.

Child learns about crickets through this hands-on encounter.

CREDIT: HUMMINGBIRD HILL NATURE LEARNING COLLECTIVE, REISTERSTOWN, MARYLAND.

As children share discoveries during nature play, teachers facilitate deeper learning about their emerging interests, such as geology, seen here.

CREDIT: DISCOVERY WILDERNESS SCHOOL, GRAND RAPIDS, MICHIGAN.

Experiential Learning and Nature-Based Learning

Nature-based learning goes hand in hand with experiential learning, which emphasizes that direct firsthand experience and reflection on this experience is how we learn concepts and skills. In this approach, children transform their understanding through direct experiences that spark the creation of new knowledge (Kolb 1984). This is relevant to all kinds of skill development, but nature connection certainly thrives on direct hands-on interactions in and with the natural world. There is no comparison between seeing pictures of plants and animals in a sunny meadow and the experience of standing in one. Imagine it now: The sensation of warm sun and breezes on your skin, the scent of milkweed blossoms, the screech of a hawk as it swoops overhead, the swishy crinkle of dry grasses as it bends and gives way underfoot, the vibrant shades of leafy green and gold against an impossibly blue sky. The experience of being in such a place—including the aesthetic and intangible aspects of being outdoors—cannot be replicated by secondhand experience on a flat, two-dimensional image or digital screen. Experiential learning invites curiosity and wonder when it takes place in sensory-rich natural outdoor environments.

to what the children are currently interested in, making learning less relevant and meaningful to children. That said, there are times when teacher-directed learning is essential—for example, when providing clear instructions on safety routines or how to properly use a tool. Some skills are learned sequentially and may require a teacher to provide direct instruction, either to individuals or as a group. When teacher-directed learning is applied, educators use it judiciously before returning focus on child-directed learning and play.

There is a push and pull between the balance of teacher-directed and child-directed learning. Following the lead of the child is always the primary mode of delivery for nature-based education. Only after considering a child's interests, background, and needs—paired with keen observation of seasonal cues—would a teacher then develop plans to facilitate learning experiences.

Table 3.1 contrasts what children may learn from teacher-directed and child-directed approaches. The table illustrates that while both approaches result in hands-on learning, the child-directed approach opens possibilities for more dynamic inquiry that encompasses several skills and values while following the children's interests. For this reason, nature-based programs emphasize child-directed learning and play to welcome broader, often more flexible and authentic opportunities for discovery.

The Simplicity of Nature Play

In the context of nature-based education, could play-based learning be as simple as exploring a grassy edge along a fence? Tossing maple seeds beneath an old maple tree? Mimicking squirrels preparing a winter cache? Observing robins having a worm

This inquisitive child has muddy investigations during a typical day of Forest Kindergarten.

CREDIT: THE WALDORF SCHOOL OF BALTIMORE, MARYLAND.

Experiential learning abounds in nature-based programs, seen here as children plant seeds to grow in the garden.

CREDIT: MONTESSORI LUNA BILINGUAL MICRO SCHOOL, PIKESVILLE, MARYLAND.

Table 3.1 Comparison of Teacher-Directed and Child-Directed Approaches

Teacher Motivation	
Teacher-Directed	**Child-Directed**
Introduce a specific skill or topic outlined by curriculum or something that interests me as the teacher.	*Children demonstrate skills, interests, or seasonal happenings they are interested in, working toward, or examining.*
Role of Teacher and Child	
Teacher introduces spiders by showing photos of them. Teacher discusses body parts of spiders and introduces a song to help children remember them. Class visits an outdoor area of the school yard with edge habitat where tall grass and shrubs meet trees. Teacher tells the children to look for spiders. Teacher demonstrates where to look for spiders and gives each child a magnifying glass and containers. Teacher identifies a patch of poison ivy and thorny brambles to avoid. Teacher encourages children to look for webs, notice differences between spiders, and count their body parts. Teacher helps catch spiders when children find them. Teacher shows spiders to the whole group and identifies them using a field guide. Teacher asks children to describe what they observe. Teacher reviews new learning and informally assesses what children have learned about spiders.	Class visits an outdoor area of the school yard with edge habitat where tall grass and shrubs meet trees. Teacher identifies a patch of poison ivy and thorny brambles to avoid. Children notice grasshoppers, spiders, and beetles in the tall grass. They try to catch them with their hands. Teacher provides insect guides, magnifiers, and containers for collection. Children use tools to observe, collect, identify, and compare insects and spiders, as well as plentiful seeds, leaves, and other natural loose parts in the area. Some children invent games, pretend, and move like the animals they find. Others make drawings in their nature journals or take photos of creatures they find. Children informally share and compare what they discover.
Learning Outcomes	
Children discover differences in the physical and behavioral adaptations of spiders.	Children express a range of learning modalities and interests as they explore and play in this habitat. This open-ended exploration reveals emergent learning across many play themes as children make discoveries that go beyond the topic of spiders. Children discover differences in the physical and behavioral adaptations of several invertebrates, including spiders. Children also make connections about life in this habitat through playful inquiry.

feast? Yes. Nature play need not be fussy. There are nuances to examine the value of this more deeply, but in a word, yes. It is that simple. The brilliantly simple combination of seasonal, child-directed play and thoughtful guidance from teachers is the basis for beneficial nature-based education.

There are opportunities for open-ended, unstructured nature play everywhere! A dandelion growing in a sidewalk crack. An overgrown, grassy edge along a fence. A wet clump of seaweed along the shore. A line of ants marching up a tree trunk. A dove cooing from a building ledge. An azalea bush in bloom. Many moments are easily overlooked, but with a renewed focus on nature play, even the most common occurrences can become opportunities for meaningful nature-based learning.

These opportunities for open-ended play in nature create the right for children to engage in meaningful learning experiences. For many teachers it is tempting to rely soley on picture books, posters, or screens to share nature with children, but nature play is not an abstraction found in picture books or posters featuring wildlife in faraway places. When teachers rely on a two-dimensional depiction of nature, the natural world seems like a distant, exotic travel destination. Children are passive in these experiences, and they are swiped away just as quickly as they are introduced. Instead, meaningful nature play can happen right outside your door. This places value on relationships with nature in the children's own community. It also highlights the amazing subtleties that are found in nature, no matter where we live. Nature play should offer direct, experiential, firsthand encounters in and with nature. By doing so, children experience nature as active participants, not as bystanders.

Children engage deeply in imaginative play with loose parts.

CREDIT: DISCOVERY WILDERNESS SCHOOL, GRAND RAPIDS, MICHIGAN.

Nature play, and all the learning that unfolds as a result, is concrete. Experiential. Direct. Firsthand. You can experience it with your senses. You can know it and feel it because you are an active participant, experiencing and influencing learning in nature or with natural treasures from outdoors. Nature play invites children to interact with elements of nature and follow their urges to explore, examine, create, and make meaning through their play. During nature play, children make both personal connections with nature as well as collective understandings when they experience nature play with others. This opens possibilities for nature connection that is directed by the child's own instincts rather than a prescribed topic or activity directed by a teacher.

Your Rhythm of the Day

This child constructs a world all their own using cut-tree sections often called "tree cookies."

CREDIT: PRAIRIEWOOD FOREST SCHOOL AT ST. FRANCIS OF THE WOODS, COYLE, OKLAHOMA.

There is so much to be accomplished each day that it may seem difficult to find time for unstructured nature play. A "Rhythm of the Day," also called a "daily rhythm," is a flexible framework but *not* a tightly prescribed timetable for learning. While children find comfort knowing what comes next by having a daily schedule, a daily rhythm allows for a predictable sequence of experiences without rigid time constraints. For example, if children are deeply engaged in imaginative play around shelter building, with a flexible framework there is no pressure to cut their experience short because of an arbitrary need to shift activities on a schedule.

Take a look at your existing schedule or daily rhythm. Consider what activities and experiences are a priority. How do you spend the balance of your time with the children? How much time is allotted for transitions, snacks, and toileting, for example? How much time is available for unstructured, open-ended play? How much learning is planned in advance and determined by the teachers? How much learning takes place indoors versus outdoors? Active versus seated? How much choice and independence do children have in their learning experiences throughout the day? Think about what works well and what changes could have a positive effect on nature-based learning.

The following sample daily rhythm outlines what a typical day of a nature-based preschool may look like. Remember, this is but one example and is not meant to be a cookie cutter for how other nature-based programs must operate! Feel free to use and modify this sample as you determine a daily rhythm that works for your program.

Sample Rhythm of the Day

Class time: 8:30 a.m. to 2 p.m.

Ages: 3–5 years old

7:30 a.m.–8:30 a.m.	Teachers arrive, perform daily site scan, connect about the day's experiences, and prepare and arrange materials before children arrive.
8:30 a.m.–9:00 a.m.	Informal arrival time with sign-in procedures. Children use the potty, wash their hands, go through opening routines (e.g., place name stone in the basket, hang up backpack, find name tag), and slowly warm up to the day.
9:00 a.m.–9:45 a.m.	Children freely choose what they would like to do; **invitations** are available for open-ended nature play. (*Note*: An invitation is a thoughtful, often beautiful, arrangement of materials that invite children to explore and combine them in their own ways. An invitation to play is a concept derived from the Reggio Emilia approach that encourages children to learn through exploration. A provocation is the new learning that is provoked or stimulated within the child as a result of an invitation. Although the terms "invitation" and "provocation" are closely related and are often used interchangeably, they do have different meanings: The *invitation* is presented by the teacher, and the *provocation* is what transpires when children interact through playful exploration.)
9:45 a.m.	Auditory cue/chant to clean up and store materials, followed by a transition to a Circle Gathering, Morning Meeting, or something similar. (A visual cue can also be helpful.)
9:45 a.m.–10:00 a.m.	Circle Gathering. Teachers lead a welcome song followed by a mindful gratitude practice. Children share thoughts during talking/listening time, which may include guided questions such as "What do you notice?" or "What do you wonder?" Teachers can share an interactive activity informed by seasonal happenings, children's interests, or skill development. Activities might include storytelling, science experiments, artifact sharing, songs, and games.

(*Continued*)

Sample Rhythm of the Day (*Continued*)

10:00 a.m.	Cue for transition. Children get gear for a nature walk and hydrate with water. They carry their own backpacks with water, a snack, and extra gear as needed (e.g., spare mittens or hat).
10:00 a.m.–11:30 a.m.	Children explore, wander, and engage in nature play. Teachers supervise, observe, and document learning. Teachers may incorporate additional tools, materials, or games to further the children's interests, skill development, or nature connection. Snack time may take place at any time with handwashing or hand sanitizer procedures.
11:30 a.m.–12:00 p.m.	Cue for transition. Children wash hands/use hand sanitizer, share gratitude for food, and enjoy lunch together.
12:00 p.m.–12:30 p.m.	Reflection time. Children do storytelling, nature journaling, or art experiences as they think about today's activities.
12:30 p.m.–1:30 p.m.	Cue for transition. Children go potty and move to a covered outdoor napping area. Transition may include guided visual imagery or story as children settle in for naps. Quiet activities are offered as needed.
1:30 p.m.	Cue for transition. Teachers offer a song to gently wake everyone. Children pack up gear and items that need to be laundered.
1:45 p.m.	Sit Spot routine.
1:50 p.m.–2:00 p.m.	Closing Circle. Children offer thoughts inspired during their (outdoor) Sit Spot. They reflect on and share stories from the day's experiences. Teachers record highlights with the heading "Ask me about …" to share at pick up. Session ends with closing gratitude and goodbye song.
2:00 p.m.	Dismissal/pick-up with sign-out procedures (e.g., children gather belongings, hang up their name tag, parents sign out their children, teachers share "Ask me about" chalkboard).
2:00 p.m.–3:00 p.m.	Teachers debrief about the day's experiences, document additional anecdotes, and consider how children's experiences today will inform tomorrow's lessons. Teachers clean up, care for and store materials, and properly dispose of waste as needed.

Teachers observe and document learning throughout the day which informs emergent curriculum. See Chapter 3 appendix for details.

As you can see from the example, the rhythm of the day is a useful framework that includes key aspects of each day (e.g., handwashing, eating, toileting, napping) with swaths of time that hold space for open-ended, child-directed nature play. You can easily shift based on the energy, interests, and needs of the children, which allows teachers to flex and flow based on the needs of the group.

NOTE: *Your daily rhythm may include campfires, special guests, or community chores, and is applicable to both indoor and outdoor settings. Feel free to modify this rhythm to suit your learning community.*

The 50/50 Principle

When planning your daily rhythm, you might implement the 50/50 principle (Young et al. 2010). That is, if 50 percent of the day includes predetermined teacher-directed activities, then the other 50 percent of the day allows for unstructured, open-ended exploration to see where the learning will take you. In nature-based early childhood education programs, the unstructured portion of the day translates into child-directed activities and experiences via nature-based invitations, exploration in nature/green spaces, and outdoor nature play. The 50/50 principle is merely a suggestion, however, and the percentages of time can (and should!) fluctuate depending on the learning community's needs and interests.

Nature-Based Learning and Play in Action

Given the trifecta of time, space, and permission for unstructured nature play, children spontaneously engage their senses and their whole bodies. They drive their own direct experiences with the environment as nature-based learning unfolds.

These playful behaviors are commonly observed during open-ended nature play. How do you facilitate these behaviors outdoors and link them to your curriculum?

Wonder, question, predict.

CREDIT: PRAIRIEWOOD FOREST SCHOOL AT ST. FRANCIS OF THE WOODS, COYLE, OKLAHOMA.

Notice, observe.

CREDIT: FALLS CHURCH–MCLEAN CHILDREN'S CENTER, FALLS CHURCH, VIRGINIA.

Tinker, experiment, manipulate.

CREDIT: BLUESTONE VILLAGE AND NATURE PROGRAMS, SHOHOLA, PENNSYLVANIA.

Invent, create, construct.

CREDIT: MONTESSORI LUNA BILINGUAL MICRO SCHOOL, PIKESVILLE, MARYLAND.

Wander, explore.

CREDIT: LIVE & LEARN EARLY LEARNING CENTER, LEE, NEW HAMPSHIRE.

Imagine, pretend, dream.

CREDIT: HUMMINGBIRD HILL NATURE LEARNING COLLECTIVE, REISTERSTOWN, MARYLAND.

Search, research.

CREDIT: GOOSEBERRY NATURE SCHOOL, COVINGTON, KENTUCKY.

Consider, compare, evaluate.

CREDIT: EPIPHANY PRESCHOOL, VIENNA, VIRGINIA.

Listen, explain, describe.

CREDIT: DISCOVERY WILDERNESS SCHOOL, GRAND RAPIDS, MICHIGAN.

Name, identify.

CREDIT: EPIPHANY PRESCHOOL, VIENNA, VIRGINIA.

Tend, protect.

CREDIT: BLUESTONE VILLAGE AND NATURE PROGRAMS, SHOHOLA, PENNSYLVANIA.

Thank, appreciate.

CREDIT: LIVE & LEARN EARLY LEARNING CENTER, LEE, NEW HAMPSHIRE.

Chapter 3

Challenge, defend.

CREDIT: THE WALDORF SCHOOL OF BALTIMORE, MARYLAND.

Negotiate, compromise, forgive.

CREDIT: GOOSEBERRY NATURE SCHOOL, COVINGTON, KENTUCKY.

Feel, inspire.

CREDIT: HUMMINGBIRD HILL NATURE LEARNING COLLECTIVE, REISTERSTOWN, MARYLAND.

Fail, persevere.

CREDIT: BLUESTONE VILLAGE AND NATURE PROGRAMS, SHOHOLA, PENNSYLVANIA.

Harvest, celebrate, honor.

Reflect.

CREDIT: ASSOCIATION FOR NATURE-BASED EDUCATION, NOTCHCLIFF NATURE PROGRAMS, GLEN ARM, MARYLAND.

Each of these descriptors may seem simplistic and obvious at first glance, but they are at the heart of how children engage in playful nature-based learning. The lived experience of play is an evolving process, one that helps children construct and reveal their understanding about the world. There are many ways to interpret how this list of experiences could manifest in nature-based programs, and there are certainly many other behaviors we could include. The point is that these experiences are child directed, deeply meaningful, and compatible with any developmentally appropriate curriculum. These experiences are flexible, involve the senses, and leave room for children to make choices concerning their interactions with nature and with others. Endless learning, across developmental domains, is possible from this little list.

These behaviors demonstrate what children do given time, space, and permission to play and learn outside, making personal connections with the land and each other.

**The Importance of Unstructured Play for Children with Disabilities
By Hannah Gallagher, MEd, Inclusive Programs Director**

Seattle Children's PlayGarden, Seattle, Washington

Unstructured play is a key element for every child's development. During unstructured play, kids ignite their creativity and develop their problem-solving and motor-planning skills. They are able to explore their surroundings, process new information, relax, dream, think, and move at the pace that is right for them at that moment.

Despite the benefits of unstructured play, children with disabilities have far fewer opportunities for unstructured play than their peers without disabilities. Persistent exclusion, stigma, intense therapy schedules, and the misconception that children with disabilities always need to be "learning something" are a few reasons why free play is limited.

Families of children with disabilities face judgment, stigma, and isolation when visiting public parks and playgrounds and while attending community events. They also face exclusion from early childhood programs, including nature-based preschools. It is often because of these barriers that parents of children with disabilities feel they need to be extra protective of their children. Parents have expressed a strong need to stay extra close to their children in case something happens, to advocate for their child, and to help them navigate play and social interactions.

Children with disabilities move through mind-boggling days filled with school, therapy, medical appointments, and tutoring. Their lives are highly scheduled from the time they start early intervention services all the way through their schooling. Almost every part of this busy schedule is adult-directed time, and by their very nature these parts of a child's day (such as therapy) are work for the child. Children with disabilities are asked to listen and respond to adult direction all day, every day. They are often asked to correct their behavior and their language or pay more attention to their bodies. Although this intervention comes from a good place, there are times when adult intervention or support can limit a child's autonomy and independence. This schedule leaves very little time for a child with a disability to simply be a kid and to play.

Teachers can also fall into ableist teaching traps that further limit access to unstructured play. For example, a teacher may believe the dangerous misconception that their students with disabilities are in some way or form "behind" their peers and therefore assume the child will benefit from more adult intervention. However, adult intervention with subtle directions such as "Hold the shovel like this" or "Not like that, this is how you put the dress-up on" interrupts the child's play.

(*Continued*)

The Importance of Unstructured Play for Children with Disabilities
By Hannah Gallagher, MEd, Inclusive Programs Director (*Continued*)

Teachers may also believe the misconception that all children with disabilities are fragile or that they need to be taught how to play and are in need of constant physical or emotional support. This constant support limits the child's sense of agency, confidence, independence, and opportunities to make friends and take risks. With this mindset, it is easy to forget that kids are kids, first and foremost, and just because a child has a disability doesn't mean that they don't benefit from risky play or mastering a new physical skill like jumping off high things on their own. Space has to be given for all children to grow.

As early childhood educators, we can do our part to remove these barriers by changing the way we think about disability, accessibility, and who nature-based programs are designed for. We can begin to shift our attitudes, practices, and beliefs to pave the way toward true inclusion and acceptance.

The Seattle Children's PlayGarden was created in response to exactly these kinds of barriers. The vision was to create a beautiful place where families could bring their kids—with and without disabilities—to simply play in an environment that was safe, welcoming, and inclusive. Since 2013, the PlayGarden has operated a fully inclusive outdoor preschool program for children with and without disabilities ages 3 through 6 years old.

At PlayGarden preschool the students spend over half their school day in unstructured, child-directed outdoor free play in the sun, rain, ice, and snow. We allow the children to stay in their play for long periods of time, explore a variety of different materials, and guide themselves through the garden on their own free will. Naturally, they become gardeners, builders, artists, engineers, scientists, and so much more. Through their play, they become caretakers and stewards. They learn how to take care of our resident chickens, ducks, and rabbits along with the wild animals we encounter on a daily basis. The students grow a deep appreciation for the garden and for each other. Ensuring that every child is given opportunities for unstructured playtime is key to the success of our inclusive model.

In the photos, we can see different children doing various things during their playtime. Jaden may choose to organize the watering cans as a way to calm himself down, as an absent-minded thing to do with his hands while he thinks about other things, or maybe it is a way for him to practice his pouring skills or a way to practice making a pattern, or maybe it is all of those things simultaneously. As adults, we do not know exactly what these behaviors are doing for the child, but we can assume that they are doing something positive for their growth, and therefore it is important we make the time for this kind of play on a daily basis.

To see examples of what unstructured play can look like for children with and without disabilities in a nature-based program, we invite you to visit the PlayGarden and watch a few of their videos on our YouTube channel: https://www.youtube.com/channel/UCfXq0FMZKOqyXrePGb1HrkA.

A young girl with autism plays with lavender in a whiskey barrel.

CREDIT: SEATTLE CHILDREN'S PLAYGARDEN.

A young boy with autism plays with watering cans during free play.

CREDIT: SEATTLE CHILDREN'S PLAYGARDEN.

Loose Parts Play with Natural Materials

Children have been imitating, exploring, manipulating, and playing with materials found in nature for as long as people have existed. Simon Nicholson's "Theory of Loose Parts" helped bring the value of loose parts play to light: "In any environment, both the degree of inventiveness and creativity, and the possibility of discovery, are directly proportional to the number and kind of variables in it" (Nicholson 1971, 30). Simply put, Nicholson's theory highlights the role of a learning environment with variables that children can manipulate in new ways.

Nature provides a sensory backdrop with endless variables (loose parts) for children to manipulate. The greater the variety of materials, the more combinations there are for children to discover. Nature is generous and many different materials are plentiful. The benefits of loose parts play are evident from the outside in (bringing natural materials indoors) and from the inside out (moving activities and experiences outside). In both cases, children become familiar and comfortable with available natural materials and gain greater appreciation for the local environment where they originate.

As you consider how to inspire and scaffold children's learning through play, loose parts are ideal to include in nature-based education. The materials listed in the following table may be a useful place to start.

Table 3.2 Materials for Loose Parts Play

Natural Loose Parts	Recycled or Repurposed Loose Parts	Tools or Other Supplies
Seeds and seed pods (e.g., acorns, pine cones)	Plastic containers and lids	Field guides
Twigs and branches	Paper bags	Maps
Leaves	Paper tubes	Magnifier, loupe, or magnifying boxes
Evergreen needles	Cardboard and tagboard boxes or pizza box lids	Binoculars or monocular
Palm fronds	Beverage jugs and cartons	Spotting scope
Flowers, flowerheads, and petals	Spice jars	Microscope or portable microscope
Grass, dried grasses	Spray bottles	Unlined journal
Stones	Fabric remnants or scraps	Drawing, writing, painting implements
Corn cobs and husks	Yarn or ribbon scraps	Scissors
Bones and skulls	Kitchen items (e.g., bowls, pans, strainers, spoons)	Taxidermy specimens of birds, insects, or other animals
Wool, fur, and hides	Corks	Paracord or nylon cord
Feathers and bird eggshells	Bricks	Replica bones or skulls
Tree "cookies" (cut slices from tree trunk or tree branches)	Flowerpots	Preserved nests or eggs
Tree bark	Wooden clothes pins	Galvanized metal pails or washtubs
Straw bales	Garage items (e.g., nuts, bolts, screws, and wood scraps)	Animal track stamps
Vines (e.g., grapevine)		Embroidery needles
Moss		Ruler or tape measure
Sand		Flashlight and/or headlamp
Insect or spider molts (e.g., cicada shells)		Bandanas
Shed snakeskin		Rain gauge
Seashells		Outdoor thermometer
Icicles or blocks of ice		Bird feeders and seed
		Hand trowels and shovels
		Child-sized rakes
		Child-sized wheelbarrow or wagon
		Outdoor blankets
		Rain flies or tarps

*Consider the age and abilities of children in your group to avoid possible choking hazards.

Using and Respecting Natural Materials

If you gather materials from nature to use with loose parts play, do so with care and respect. The rule of 100 goes like this: If you can count 100 of something, it may be okay to collect *one*. Some plants are so prolific or invasive that you can collect as many as you may want—for example, garlic mustard or Japanese wineberry. Generally speaking, though, a concrete rule such as the rule of 100 helps everyone pause before taking anything from nature. Many popular loose parts are also sources of food or shelter for animals (e.g., acorns or tree bark), so we must consider our impact on other living things when we source materials from nature.

Remember to collect sparingly and help children understand that living things have their own purpose for growing and being, even if people don't understand what the purpose is. Robin Wall Kimmerer, an Indigenous scientist and author, wrote a beautiful book called *Braiding Sweetgrass: Indigenous Wisdom, Scientific Knowledge and the Teachings of Plants* (2015). In it, she describes the "honorable harvest" that is guided by principles that encourage people to ask permission before taking, leave a gift in reciprocity of what is taken, take only what is needed, and use what you take. The honorable harvest, like the rule of 100, means you don't take the first or last of anything. Kimmerer reminds us in her second book, *The Serviceberry: Abundance and Reciprocity in the Natural World*, that "Receiving a gift from the land is coupled to attached responsibilities of sharing, respect, reciprocity, and gratitude," and that "If our first response to the receipt of gifts is gratitude, then our second is reciprocity: to give a gift in return" (Kimmerer 2024, 13). This core understanding supports a child's growing environmental literacy because "how we think ripples out to how we behave" (Kimmerer 2024, 25).

Don't gather natural materials where pesticides or other harmful chemicals may be sprayed, such as roadsides. You should also avoid collecting from places where pets gather (e.g., dog parks). Always get permission from landowners before collecting, and if you are on public land, make sure you are aware of any rules against taking things home. Thanks to the Migratory Bird Treaty Act, birds are protected from collection, and the Act makes it illegal to keep their feathers unless you are part of an Indigenous tribe.

When the playful investigations are over and your documentation is complete, teach children to return natural materials to the Earth. You may do this by returning items to the compost bin or scattering materials where they were originally found. Rocks and sticks may be part of collections, but these short-term collections should eventually rotate back outdoors.

For nature discoveries that children are especially fond of or attached to, they may have a tough time returning them to nature. It can be helpful to document those special natural items by taking a photo or video so the child can revisit it without removing it from nature. Likewise, children can create a keepsake album of photos to document precious finds throughout the school year. Children may also experiment with technology such as an instant camera or a digital camera to document items or moments they want to remember. A collaborative album lends itself to sharing with families and encourages storytelling about daily adventures. Another favorite activity is to encourage children to take a "mental picture" of the natural item using a viewfinder (or hands cupped in a circle to narrow the field of vision and to better focus on the object). Taking a mental picture includes careful study of the natural item by visually tracking its shape, noticing its texture and color, and even measuring it for size. By tracing the natural object's outline or drawing it from a mental picture, children will practice visualizing the unique and memorable qualities of the natural item. As the adage goes, "Leave only footprints, take only memories." These activities will allow children to hold onto their collections, but do so in a different, more respectful way that honors nature and reinforces our role as caretakers.

Loose parts play is immensely beneficial for children. When stewardship, caretaking, and conservation are integral to learning with loose parts, children also benefit by developing a deeper, more respectful relationship with the natural world.

Supporting Risky Play and Independence in Outdoor Settings

Parents, teachers, and researchers alike have been grappling with the compelling concept of risky play for decades. After all, if there is risk involved, isn't that something to avoid? Ellen Beate Hansen Sandseter defines *risky play* as "thrilling and exciting forms of physical play that involve uncertainty and a risk of physical injury" (Sandseter 2010, 22). Research reveals that risky play provides rich opportunities for children to test their own limits and can have lasting positive outcomes.

Many of the benefits of risky play support children's physical development. In the ever-changing, unpredictable setting of nature, children move their bodies differently to navigate uneven terrain, wet or mushy earth, steep inclines, and wobbly things underfoot. As kids test the limits of their bodies, they take risks that can improve their physical skills over time.

Some examples of risky play include:

> Year-round nature walks and hikes
> Climbing on (under or over) branches, logs, or rocks
> Exploring aquatic habitats, presence of water
> Digging in soil or sand
> Climbing trees
> Running and chasing one another
> Pretend play or building that involves sticks and stones
> Hiding and camouflaging
> Touching or holding animals
> Lifting and moving heavy things (e.g., logs, rocks)
> Rolling downhill

> Swinging and spinning

> Sledding or snowshoeing in snow

> Using force to break something (e.g., to open seed pods or break apart a clump of earth)

> Tool use of all kinds (e.g., hand drill, rope, saw, hammer)

> Presence of campfire and fire making

All these activities involve direct experience in nature, and the benefits overflow into every developmental domain. Notably, social-emotional development is prominent because children gain confidence as they master new skills and collaborate with their peers (for details, see Chapter 2, "Childhood Development and the Benefits of Nature-Based Learning").

It is imperative that programs clearly define policies and protocol around risky play activities as part of their risk management procedures. This begins with a basic understanding between a "risk" and a "hazard" in the context of nature-based learning and play. A *hazard* is something that can cause death or debilitating injury, and it is the responsibility of adults to identify, prevent, and avoid and/or remove them (e.g., a wasp nest, dead branch in overhanging tree, patch of poison ivy). Hazards may be in the form of elements that are present in the physical outdoor environment (e.g., busy road or steep cliff) or as activities that a child may engage in (e.g., wading in water or using a saw). In terms of risky play, a *risk* is an activity or experience with a chance of injury or harm that can be mitigated with adult support. Risky play differs from hazards because there is potential for a developmentally appropriate risk that the child can choose to engage in (or not), and there is a development benefit if they do choose to participate. For example, if a child is afraid that they cannot safely walk across a log, the educator may offer to hold their hand as they try or ask if they would like to choose a different activity, thus allowing the child to make a choice about taking this risk.

The reason programs choose to engage in risky play is because there are significant benefits, but it is up to each program and educator to know their children well to determine acceptable risks compared to its potential benefits (this is known as a "Risk Benefit Assessment"). Families also need to understand what risky play looks like in your program and sign a waiver to acknowledge the inherent risks and benefits of nature play.

When we provide space for children to experiment with risk, we honor their growing independence and capacity to make choices about which risks they want to take. In 2009, Sandseter's research described several characteristics of risky play, which were further elaborated on by her and a colleague in 2019 (Sandseter 2009; Sandseter & Kleppe 2019).

Findings from this research indicate that risky play allows children to "learn risk assessment and how to master risk situations and thus develop a sound sense of risk which may aid survival when, later in life, watchful

NOTE: *Allowing risky play does not eliminate the need to set boundaries, engage in daily safety routines, and give explicit instruction about safety expectations. Each program must define appropriate risky play behaviors for their program and distinguish between environmental hazards and dangerous activities. Risk management should include thorough emergency planning and Risk Benefit Assessment (see Chapter 5, "Visioning and Managing a Nature-Based Program").*

adults are no longer present" (Sandseter 2009, 7). Sandseter also explains that children "progressively encounter risky play and seek out thrills in a gradual manner which allows them to master the challenges" (Sandseter 2009, 7). This means that children scaffold their own skills based on what risks they choose to take, in their own developmental sequence. While the idea of risky play may seem counterintuitive, unstructured nature play is in fact a major benefit of outdoor learning. It offers rich opportunities for independent, risky play alongside watchful teachers who can help children take supported risks as needed.

Building off Sandseter's findings, one study of 6- to 8-year-olds identified additional risky play categories. *Risky constructing* involves the use of tools to build something, such as a fort or hideout (Hinchion et al. 2021). Not surprisingly, another form of risky play is *breaking the rules*. Invariably, children must weigh the possible benefits of doing something they are "not allowed to do" with the consequence of breaking said rule (Hinchion et al. 2021). These examples suggest that risky play categories evolve as children age and may not be limited to the categories described here (Hinchion et al. 2021).

A nearby arboretum partnered with a Title 1 public school in Philadelphia to provide this incredible outdoor classroom space for a weekly Forest Days Outdoor Learning Program, which was offered to kindergarten students and their teachers.

CREDIT: ASSOCIATION FOR NATURE-BASED EDUCATION.

Risky play has benefits because of the many skills it can involve: bravery, problem solving, trial and error, failure, perseverance, cooperation, and confidence, to name but a few. As Angela Hanscom explains in her book *Balanced and Barefoot*, "children develop strength, coordination, resilience, problem-solving skills, and confidence when they are allowed to take risks" (Hanscom 2016).

It is also no small thing to trust a child. When children are afforded the freedom to take risks, it communicates that teachers trust in their abilities. It also provides opportunities for children to develop self-confidence as they scaffold a wide range of skills. To return to our example of walking on a log, rather than a teacher cautioning "Watch out! Be careful, that's wobbly!" the teacher can instead quietly watch as the child slowly navigates the terrain independently. The teacher might remain a silent observer or offer support: "I'm here if you need me" or "What's your plan to climb over that log?" Each of the latter phrases offer support for the child to take

Table 3.3 Categories of Risky Play

Categories	Risk	Subcategories
Great heights	Danger of injury from falling	Climbing Jumping from still or flexible surfaces Balancing on high objects Hanging/swinging at great heights
High speed	Uncontrolled speed and pace that can lead to collision with something (or someone)	Swinging at high speed Sliding and sledding at high speed Running uncontrollably at high speed Bicycling at high speed Skating and skiing at high speed
Dangerous tools	Can lead to injuries and wounds	Knives, saws, axes, hammers, ropes, twine, etc.
Dangerous elements	Where children can fall into or from something	Cliffs, steep slopes, and rocky areas Deep water or icy water Fire pits
Rough and tumble	Where the children can harm each other	Wrestling Fencing with sticks Play fighting
Disappear/get lost	Where the children can disappear from the supervision of adults, get lost alone	Go exploring alone Playing alone in unfamiliar environments
Play with impact	Children crashing into something repeatedly just for fun	Children repeatedly crash their tricycles, wagons, wheelbarrows, or other wheeled toys into the fence, a wall, or each other
Vicarious play	Children experiencing thrill by watching other children (most often older) engaging in risk	Where the observing child shows clear signs of being exhilarated by what they observe

Sources: Sandseter 2009; Sandseter & Kleppe 2019; Sandseter et al. 2021.

the risk without stirring up fear, anxiety, or self-doubt. If the teacher remains silent, it leaves space for other children to offer help or ideas, opening the possibility for social development and group problem solving.

When children have time to engage in unstructured nature play, which often leads to risky play, there are greater possibilities for children to direct their own learning. As Helen Tovey explains, "such play can thrive in the more open, flexible, diverse, and indeterminate nature of the outdoor environment where children have greater space, freedom of movement, choice and control" (Tovey 2007). Choice and independence go hand in hand! After all, risky play helps develop children's independence and autonomy (Hinchion et al. 2021). Young children are capable of being independent! They can carry their own backpacks, put on and take off their own gear, and learn to care for other classroom and outdoor supplies. Every child needs time to learn how to do these tasks on their own, but they are capable of much more than we often give them credit for. A favorite saying is "We can do hard things!"

Play is central to child development, and dually so where nature-based education is concerned. As you explore ways to facilitate nature play and support risk-taking, use this chapter as a reference to ensure that children's development blossoms through outdoor nature-based learning.

Children develop social-emotional skills through nature play, seen here as children problem-solve together while building a shelter with fallen branches.

CREDIT: ASSOCIATION FOR NATURE-BASED EDUCATION.

Joy in the Forest

The Association for Nature-Based Education (ANBE) had the great pleasure of sponsoring the Forest Days Outdoor Learning Program with two Title 1 public schools in the heart of Philadelphia, Pennsylvania, over the span of five years. The Forest Days facilitators worked with the kindergarten teachers to implement an emergent curriculum in the forest each week, either at a nearby park or directly on the school grounds.

One cold autumn day, I joined Forest Days as an observer. After the opening gathering, the children fanned out to climb over logs, collect sticks and seeds, build with branches, dig, or rake leaves. I couldn't help noticing a boy who was enthralled with the thick layer of fallen leaves that covered the forest floor. He instinctively dove into the leaves, wiggling and scooting through them. He would pause, look around, then continue to writhe and belly crawl through the leaves. This went on for nearly 45 minutes! In this example, this child had an unparalleled opportunity to learn about the warmth that leaves can provide, develop his motor skills, and engage his senses through outdoor nature play.

When the facilitator, kindergarten teachers, and I met to debrief later, we noted that there would be no way for this child to fulfill his apparent developmental need to move his body inside the classroom. In fact, he would have been chastised for trying to do so. Children's behavior reveals what they are interested in and can show us the skills they actively need to develop. This is true of social-emotional skills as well as physical and cognitive skills. In this case, there was an instinct to move! During each session, the children we observed had a complex range of skill development that we could map back to curriculum standards. It may be unconventional, but the learning taking place was real. Given the opportunity for unstructured nature play, meaningful skill development emerged as children grew to love the forest.

Children discover what's under all those leaves while they dig and play.

CREDIT: ASSOCIATION FOR NATURE-BASED EDUCATION.

Appendix: Nature Play and Emergent Curriculum: Perfect Partners

As discussed in the chapter, the natural environment offers many opportunities for educators to introduce content and stimulate skill development to support curricular goals. Because the natural world is always moving and changing, nature play can be a springboard for an emergent curriculum. In nature-based early childhood education, *emergent curriculum* is an ongoing collaborative process by which children explore their own ideas as they interact in a natural learning environment to construct meaning. Teachers observe, document, and nurture children's interests and ideas as they emerge through a combination of unstructured and/or teacher-guided play, which are then supported by intentional activities that deepen learning to align with curricular goals and standards. Emergent curriculum is a way to co-create meaningful curriculum in collaboration with children, teachers, and the learning community, including the natural world.

This approach is beloved by many early childhood educators because children's ideas are honored through self-directed, open-ended play and intrinsic motivation (Jones 2012). When curriculum is too tightly structured and teacher directed, it can stifle growth. Notes Mary Ann Biermeier, "A standardized curriculum that is designed to replicate outcomes often eliminates all possibility of spontaneous inquiry, stealing potential moments of learning from students and teachers in a cookie-cutter approach to education" (2015, 74). By contrast, emergent curriculum is co-created with children. The concept of co-creating a curriculum through a process of observation, documentation, and in response to children's ideas is revolutionary for teachers who have been trained to work with children in a traditional, teacher-directed manner. As Biermeier asserts, "It is a perspective that turns structured curriculum, with predetermined outcomes, on its head" (2015, 74). Susan Stacey, a highly regarded expert in emergent curriculum in early childhood education, points out that "When teachers are limited to a repetitive, mundane curriculum, it is almost impossible to maintain energy and enthusiasm—much less passion—for their work" (Stacey 2018, 3). In contrast, emergent curriculum opens possibilities that allow teachers to acknowledge and pursue the many diverse interests and abilities of the children and "remember the potential of the child"

How far can I jump? Questions like this emerge through nature play and can form the basis of an emergent curriculum.

CREDIT: ASSOCIATION FOR NATURE-BASED EDUCATION.

Teachers listen to children's ideas and incorporate them into documentation that helps inform emergent curriculum.

CREDIT: MONTESSORI LUNA BILINGUAL MICRO SCHOOL, PIKESVILLE, MARYLAND.

without tightly prescribed or scripted curriculum (Stacey 2018, 3).

For those who are new to emergent curriculum, there may be confusion between what we know about intentional planning to support developmentally appropriate practices and how to harness learning that emerges through play. Wang and Delfin aptly note that "intentional interactions and deliberate design often start with a focus on teaching with planning; in other words, teaching follows purposefully designed lesson plans and activities and reflects intentional assessments and tasks," which offers structure to the curriculum (Wang & Delfin 2024, 910). So how do educators engage in planning while embracing the open-ended, spontaneous nature of emergent curriculum through child's play?

Observation and Documentation

Observation and documentation are essential to planning an emergent curriculum. If children's ideas and discoveries from nature provide the spark for learning, then observations and documentation are the means to fuel the fire. By observing children at play, educators gain insight that helps them support the children's interests and development.

Information gathered as documentation during observations is used as data to decode what children are interested in and actively pursuing. Observations ignite teacher responses with additional activities and experiences that can help guide skill development.

Observations, and supporting documentation that make learning visible, may be carried out in several formats. The following list includes various methods for documentation:

> Notes and logs (e.g., handwritten journal, digital document, or voice-to-text notes on your phone), which may be taken for individual children and for group activities or social play.

> Photographs that document skills, interactions, inquiry, and stages in the learning process. These are not meant to be marketing photos with children smiling at the camera but rather photos that reveal steps in the learning process, ideally from the child's vantage point.

> Written or audio dictation by teacher or child that describes what is happening in photos.

> Video clips that document learning experiences, provide context for learning, and, in some cases, narration of what is taking place.

> Transcripts of conversations (Stacey 2023).

> Artifacts ("traces of children's work") such as mark-making in nature journals or drawings, patterning, built structures, and other remnants of manipulated materials provide a crumb trail of clues about what children are interested in, what they can do, and ideas they are exploring through play (Stacey 2018).

> Portfolios as a collection of work samples and artifacts that help demonstrate a child's growth and development of learning processes over time.

> Seasonal nature notes or phenology journals documenting specific occurrences that happen in nature—for example, when children see the first hummingbird return or when the first frost covers the ground.

> Digital apps such as Storypark are designed for documentation that enables teachers to upload photos, videos, and documents to share among colleagues and with families. Teachers can also track which learning standards apply to documented activities, and others can give feedback through written, audio, or video replies.

> Exhibits and displays make the children's artifacts, paired with documentation, visible and accessible. Sometimes called "documentation panels," these should be placed at the children's eye level so they can continue to interact and reflect on their experiences.

> Changeable books allow teachers and children to view photos and dictation as desired into readily available books that children can play with. These books provide opportunities for children to keep exploring ideas that have been documented (e.g., a small 4 x 6 photo book can include color printouts of photos, or a binder with plastic sleeves can serve as a changeable format for documentation).

> Learning Stories, an approach created by Margaret Carr and Wendy Lee, two New Zealand early childhood researchers, are narratives written for individual children that highlight specific play or interactions the child engages in (Stacey 2023).

> Floorbooks are collaborative documentation tools developed by Claire Warden, founder of Auchlone Nature Kindergarten in Scotland and consultant to countless others. Children can use Floorbooks for drawing, mark-making, mapping, and other forms of reflection as they explore their interests (Stacey 2023; Warden 1995).

An invitation with ice can provoke all kinds of inquiry during winter nature play.

CREDIT: THE WALDORF SCHOOL OF BALTIMORE, MARYLAND.

However, to be able to understand what the observations may mean, nature-based educators must come to their work prepared with knowledge about child development, environmental literacy, and safety practices as they relate to outdoor learning (for more on this, see Chapters 4 and 5). For example, children who are engaged in a nature play experience of rolling seeds down a hill may be attaining several overlapping skills (e.g., understanding gravity and velocity, learning about seed adaptations, applying language to express ideas, making predictions, trial-and-error tinkering, and regulating emotions while socializing with peers). If an educator cannot readily identify the many skills they are observing in this example of nature play, they are likely to miss its value. Observations are a form of research that reveals areas of growth alongside a child's interests, and the more time and practice educators have documenting observations, the more skilled educators become at noticing trends and gaps in learning. Equipped with a sound understanding of developmentally appropriate skills and practices, educators can translate nature play experiences into skill development and consider how to deepen learning that is relevant to curricular goals and standards. In this way, educators observe and document the interests, backgrounds, and abilities of the children alongside seasonal happenings in the outdoor learning environment, which continues the cycle of co-creating emergent curriculum (Stacey 2018).

Understanding Emergent Curriculum Through Nature Play

Emergent curriculum provides a framework that supports the emergent learning that takes place. It keeps the focus on children learning through play, and when infused with nature-based learning, it provides another level of learning and connection. Children are viewed as capable of constructing knowledge with the support of flexible, creative teachers in emergent curriculum (Biermeier 2015). Child-directed interactions result in a cycle of co-created experiences with nature and those in the learning community to form the basis of the curriculum. In a nature-based emergent curriculum, ideas are sparked by:

› Children! Their ideas, prior knowledge, and experiences come to the forefront through nature play, demonstrating what they are interested in learning and doing.

› The physical, natural learning environment, which includes seasonal happenings and natural features of the landscape.

› Interactions with elements of nature, including local habitats, plants, animals, rocks, fungi, soil, water, fire, and weather.

› Interactions with others, such as classmates, teachers, parents, siblings, and community members.

› Open-ended invitations with materials (i.e., artifacts, books, and tools) that encourage or deepen children's ideas, skills, and values.

› Individual reflection based on the child's unique background, abilities, and experiences.

With this in mind, "Teachers actively seek out and chase the interests of the children" to facilitate emergent curriculum (Biermeier 2015, 73).

NOTE: *In fully immersive, outdoor nature-based childcare settings, educators take care to display documentation that is easy to transport and access in all weather settings.*

In nature-based early childhood education, children need opportunities for nature play as a natural entry point for emergent curriculum. For example, if the children have noticed petals falling from a magnolia tree in their outdoor space, then the educator may scaffold a response based on this seasonal interest. The educator may have any number of responses that could scaffold learning based on what is known about the class of children. The educator might incorporate a few fading magnolia blossoms in the mud kitchen for further examination during social play or create a tray of spring flowers for comparison, then lead a nature walk to learn more about flowering trees in the area. The educator may offer magnolia seed pods in a "nature museum" with magnifiers or digital microscopes and tweezers to allow children to examine them. Maybe the children will invent a story about why the petals fell to the ground, which could lead to an investigation of wind and rain in springtime. Children may dance like petals falling from the tree or look more closely at the blossoms to discover pollinators or birds nesting there. From this *one instance* of an observation—children noticing a change in their environment of fallen flower petals—the educator can then apply what she knows about the children, their abilities, and relevant learning standards to further the children's interests and respond to co-create curriculum in any number of ways.

Cycle of Planning an Emergent Curriculum

Children engage in nature play
Children explore, create, observe, experiment, invent, build, imagine, etc. independently or with others. Teachers provide time, space, and permission for nature play as they monitor, provide support, and model appropriate behavior.

Teachers observe and document
Teachers notice seasonal interests and experiences that captivate children during nature play. Teachers document play as it relates to developmentally appropriate skills and values with written notes, logs, photos, audio/video recordings, etc.

Teachers reflect on nature play
Teachers consider children's interests, backgrounds, abilities, and seasonal happenings alongside developmentally appropriate curricular goals. Teachers use tools for authentic assessment to determine areas of growth, interest, and needs.

Teachers plan NBL opportunities
Teachers plan activities and experiences that deepen and expand learning. Teachers scaffold seasonally relevant invitations/provocations, materials, and tools to create a balance of intentional teaching and emergency learning opportunities.

Access to nature and outdoor learning environments
Daily access to the natural outdoor learning environment invites direct experiences, open-ended learning opportunities, and unstructured nature play.

This graphic highlights how nature, children, and educators all work together to co-create emergent curriculum.

Cherry blossoms are often plentiful in spring and can inspire nature play.

CREDIT: MONICA WIEDEL-LUBINSKI.

Measuring tools are a wonderful addition to an outdoor invitation. You never know what children will be interested in measuring, like these woolly bear caterpillars.

CREDIT: LIVE & LEARNING EARLY LEARNING CENTER, LEE, NEW HAMPSHIRE.

The idea of planning an emergent curriculum may seem counterintuitive, so a deeper dive into the "Cycle of Planning an Emergent Curriculum," illustrated in the figure, can help break it down. You will notice that the cycle can begin in any of the stages, but *Access to Nature and Outdoor Learning Environments* is a good place to start. Children need safe, frequent access to green spaces and/or access to natural materials during indoor class time to set the stage for direct experiences with nature. In the next stage, *Children Engage in Nature Play*, children are invited to make choices about their learning through play. Remember that beautiful trifecta of time, space, and permission? Teachers provide all of these to afford opportunities for nature play, which allows spontaneous discoveries to manifest and become part of the emergent curriculum. Unstructured nature play provides the maximum amount of freedom in terms of children's autonomy and risk-taking, while teacher-guided play can also help children solve problems, offer encouragement, and provide small-group or one-on-one support. Once children are engaged in nature play, the next stage, *Teachers Observe and Document,* is when learning takes place. There are many tools that can be used in conjunction with observations and documentation, but the point is that teachers spend time noticing and describing the learning that unfolds (emerges), both for individual children as well as for the class. Documentation provides a window into the children's interests and skills as teachers move to the next stage, *Teachers Reflect on Nature Play*. Daily reflection with children as well as debriefing with co-teachers helps to identify the most meaningful threads of interest to pursue and weave into intentional plans. Observations and documentation are data that back a teacher's ideas about learning and inform the next stage, *Teachers Plan Nature-Based Learning Opportunities*. Once teachers are aware of the children's interests and know more about their development, as part of a co-created curriculum, they are ready to synthesize this information to plan intentional activities, materials, or tools that link to curricular standards and deepen learning based on children's interests, backgrounds, and abilities, in unison with seasonally relevant happenings in nature. After teachers offer these activities and experiences, the cycle continues as a process, revealing new threads of interest and inquiry in collaboration with children and nature.

This is framed as a cycle because it is possible to begin anywhere. For example, if you were to start at *Teachers Plan Nature-Based Learning Opportunities* and move into *Access to Nature and Outdoor Learning Environments*, then you can see how nature play, followed by observation and documentation, is vital to revealing whether your plans mesh with children's interests, skill development, and seasonally relevant occurrences in nature. The cycle progresses in the same way as you reflect on learning that takes place, which informs future investigations and planning.

To go back to the previous example, flower petals were used as part of an invitation to open-ended play. This invitation represents something a teacher may plan to further a seasonal interest, and at the same time further a skill or concept. For example, small balls of playdough may be arranged in a circle with a few baskets of flower petals, small twigs, and leaves that fell from a favorite flowering tree. This may satisfy a child's interest to explore spring flowers while also enhancing fine motor skills.

Sometimes learning stations are offered by teachers for hands-on play; however, the learning may be limited if teachers give set instructions to follow or projects that children must complete in a particular way. In contrast, an invitation is completely open-ended—there is no right or wrong way to use the materials there (as long as play is safe, of course). An invitation invites possibilities for children to freely pursue their ideas. There is no bell to ring or rotation that forces children to move onto something else. Children are invited to engage deeply with an invitation for as long as it sparks their interest.

With an invitation, the teacher does not instruct children about using materials (flower petals and playdough, in this case). A beautiful, thought-provoking invitation beckons the children who bring their own creativity and ideas to the materials. This allows the teacher to continue learning what interests the children, what skills and ideas they choose to pursue, and inform how the teacher may respond to deepen understanding.

Other ideas suggested with the magnolia exploration discussed earlier involve the teacher planning and leading an activity with greater intention to expand the children's knowledge about flowers or trees. Teachers must know when to offer open-ended opportunities for child-directed play, make observations about that play, and determine what to examine through documentation. In turn, they

Plentiful plants like these foxtails can be incorporated with an indoor invitation about grasses and seeds.

CREDIT: MONICA WIEDEL-LUBINSKI.

decide how to respond to scaffold learning, which may include teacher-guided activities such as a nature walk or science experiment. For these reasons, observations and documentation of learning are a vital part of the planning process for teachers. This is how play can reveal the children's interests and abilities, and inform which seasonal elements, skills, values, and ideas to pursue to co-create an emergent curriculum.

> ### The Reggio Emilia Approach: Atelier
>
> Many educators are inspired by Louis Malaguzzi's approaches from childcare programs in Reggio Emilia, Italy. Similar to invitations in nature-based classrooms, the *atelier* is "a space rich in materials, tools, and people with professional competencies" where children are free to "experiment with alternative modalities, techniques, instruments, and materials as teachers observe and document the process of learning" (Edwards et al. 2012, 50).

Emergent curriculum relies on "flowing and negotiable" timeframes with "no struggle against the clock" to allow children to fully explore their ideas (Wurm 2005, 52). To that end, consider your daily routines with children to create a Daily Rhythm (discussed earlier in the chapter). By incorporating a Daily Rhythm, educators and children can follow "the same predictable order but without fret," which supports the co-creation of a nature-based, child-directed emergent curriculum (Wurm 2005, 3).

Children share a quiet moment observing what's at the edge of the pond.

CREDIT: ASSOCIATION FOR NATURE-BASED EDUCATION, NOTCHCLIFF NATURE PROGRAMS.

Look for opportunities to introduce or extend open-ended nature play or nature-based invitations. Perhaps you can tweak something you already have in place. For example:

› Can you extend a free-choice time and move it outdoors?

› Can you infuse rotating stations with more natural materials and artifacts?

› Can you introduce a daily nature hour for open-ended play and inquiry?

› Can you introduce a regular nature walk with time for exploration?

› Can you incorporate a "nature minute" to share something seasonally relevant followed by time for children to explore it on their own?

› Can you stock a wagon or special tote bag with materials that encourage nature play?

› Can you share a nature-based story or song and then invite children to use these as inspiration for outdoor nature play?

Any of these will encourage children to explore nature and provide space for them to make choices about the kind of nature play they want to engage in. As you expand opportunities for child-directed nature play, you will have a greater ability to observe and document the seasonal interests, abilities, and ideas of children that form the basis of an emergent curriculum.

Flow Learning

Flow Learning is an approach articulated by Joseph Cornell in his book *Sharing Nature with Children*, first published in 1979. He describes the sequences of flow learning in four parts: awaken enthusiasm, focus attention, offer direct experience, and share inspiration. This sequence continues to inform approaches to outdoor learning with young children. In 2010, Jon Young, Ellen Haas, and Evan McGown expounded on flow learning in their approach to nature connection in *The Coyote's Guide to Connecting with Nature*. This book includes historic and cultural references to directional teaching as related to flow learning. Both of these approaches form the basis for implementation of emergent curriculum that moves between unstructured outdoor play and intentional, focused learning.

Creative arts teachers with experience in music, dance, visual art, and theater often have a heightened awareness of what it means to enjoy a flow state of learning, doing, and being. Creative use of materials, situational awareness, and observation are also useful skills that are easily applied in nature-based settings for teachers and children alike.

The Intersection of Nature-Based Education and the Reggio Emilia Approach

By Maryfaith Decker Miller, Director, The Forest Learning Collective, Cortland, New York

The Forest Learning Collective is a nature immersion program where children are outdoors 100 percent of the time, through the fall, winter, and spring. Being truly child-led means we do not write lesson plans for our kindergarten to seventh grade learning groups. What implications does that have on meeting standards? The Reggio Emilia Approach has provided the path to utilizing a fully emergent curriculum while tracking the learning happening in each learning group. We rely on the natural world's ever-changing, dynamic classroom to provide learners with mysteries to solve, curiosities to follow, and problems to research.

Once a learning group is engaged in a project, the guide steps back into the researcher role. Guides document the learning by collecting traces of conversations, artwork and drawings, and photographs and videos of the project, and writing the story of the learning. The documentation is entered into the Storypark app, where it is shared with parents of the children in the learning story. These documentations are shared with the students to help make their learning visible, to remind learners of the remaining unanswered questions, and sometimes for learners to restart a project. The app is also a data analytics tool because the learning stories can be tagged with the state standards that the guides noticed the learners had covered while engaged in their project.

Periodically, guides and the pedagogy consultant will discuss the areas of the standards that have been covered and the areas that have been missed. Then it's easy to adjust the learning environment to include provocations that help the learners move forward into those areas. For example, a kindergarten learning group report conducted midyear revealed that at no time did the children employ the standards regarding counting and cardinality. The mathematics standards in this group ask kindergartners to:

> Identify whether the number of objects in one group is greater than, less than, or equal to the number of objects in another group and compare two numbers between 1 and 10 presented as written numerals.

In addition, the kindergartners were asked to:

> Understand the relationship between numbers and quantities up to 20; connect counting to cardinality. When counting objects, say the number names in the standard order, pairing each object with one and only one number name and each

After children gather natural materials, teachers may offer an extension to further their knowledge about nature, seen here as a child sorts leaves by color.

CREDIT: EPIPHANY PRESCHOOL. VIENNA, VIRGINIA.

Hands-on learning sometimes means "toes on" learning! Here a child experiences a pond with her senses as the teacher looks on.

CREDIT: BLUESTONE VILLAGE AND NATURE PROGRAMS.

number name with one and only one object. (1:1 correspondence) (Common Core State Standards 2010)

To lead the learners into this area of thinking, we placed a gathering basket at each child's place for morning circle and relied on the natural play motif of "gathering." Younger children love to gather objects from the forest, and a natural next step is to compare them with ones their peers have found. With very little prompting, the children counted out and compared what each of them had found. Some children found some very shiny black rocks along a trail that used to be a railroad bed. These were highly regarded and soon became a currency among the learners, which touched on a social studies standard under the heading "Economics and Economic Systems." The rocks were heavy to carry, which by necessity had the learners writing down their transactions on paper, thus completing two more standards in math and social studies.

Reflection Questions

> What additional strategies might you incorporate to support emergent curriculum?
> How do teacher responsibilities support the implementation of emergent curriculum?
> What tools and practices do you use each day to document and co-create emergent curriculum?

Additional Resources

Miles, M., & Duffy, D. 2022. "A Wormery Spurs an Inquiry: Worms Throughout the Curriculum." *YC Young Children* 15 (4).

Sweeny, S.J., & Fillmore, R.M. 2018. "The Birds, the Children, and the Big Black Dog: Reflecting on Emergent Curriculum." *YC Young Children* 73 (1): 69–72. https://www.jstor.org/stable/90019484.

CALL TO ACTION

1. Plan to visit a nature-based program, such as a forest or nature preschool, to see what a typical day looks like. Note the role of the teachers in terms of their interactions with young children and with the natural environment, as well as potential risky play activities outdoors.

2. Compile a running list of nature-based activities and experiences that can be offered in the form of invitations to nature play. Consider starting with a template like Table 3.4.

By creating a list of invitations, you will have seasonal experiences that are ripe for open-ended, child-directed play to support your emergent curriculum. As children develop new interests, you can continue to grow this list.

Table 3.4 Sample Nature Play Invitations

Nature Play Invitation	Materials	Skills and Values	Related Concepts	Season	Related Books and Resources	Notes
Nature's kitchen/ mud kitchen	Pots, pans, baking sheets, bowls, spoons, measuring cups, muffin tins, mortar and pestle May rotate other items such as water, ice, soil, sand, and natural materials	Social development Science inquiry Math ideas Expressive and receptive language Symbolic play	Resourcefulness Dramatic play Perspective-taking	Year-round	*Compost Stew: An A to Z Recipe for the Earth* by Mary McKenna Siddals *Luli and the Language of Tea* by Andrea Yang *A Pumpkin Soup Story* by Helen Cooper	Incorporate seasonally relevant natural materials throughout the school year (e.g., spent magnolia blossoms in spring)
Shelter building	Piles of fallen sticks and branches	Social skills, teamwork to build a shelter Problem solving Expressing ideas Flexible thinking Large motor development moving branches Engineering a sturdy structure	Characteristics of different kinds of wood Properties of decomposing logs Knot-tying and fastening branches Dramatic play Symbolic play Animal shelters for raising young or surviving harsh weather	Year-round Relates to nesting animals, winter dens, shelter from the elements	*Look Inside: Animal Homes* by Emily Bone *Not a Stick* by Antoinette Portis *The Perfect Shelter* by Clare Helen Welsh *Where Do Animals Go in the Winter?* by Katie Daynes	If you offer piles of branches near a tree with the suggestion of one or two sticks placed in the crook of a tree, this suggestion may spark shelter building Consider items needed for fastening, if desired (e.g., paracord or twine)

Reflection Questions

› Think about the 50/50 principle. How does your daily rhythm compare?

› How do time, space, and permission play out in your program? Consider how these relate to your curricular goals, the children's interests, seasonal occurrences, and deeper appreciation for the natural world.

› How would others describe your primary mode of teaching? What aspects of your teaching style nurture meaningful nature play?

› After reviewing the loose parts list, what additional tools or materials might help you better facilitate nature play?

› How does your risk management plan incorporate risky play in outdoor settings? What else may be necessary to include or revisit?

› To what extent do children in your program engage in nature-based activities and experiences? What other strategies might help you facilitate additional nature-based learning?

CHAPTER 4

Growing Strong Nature-Based Educators

"In nature, nothing exists alone" (Carson 1962). If we take a cue from the natural world, we know that nothing in nature, including our work with children, functions in isolation. There are interconnected forces that shape a child's learning, including the child's own experiences and genetic disposition, family interactions, and a range of social, cultural, and environmental factors. To be sure, countless educators, psychologists, and researchers have pondered these relationships to better understand how children grow and learn. Where nature-based early childhood education is concerned, we pause to consider how teachers provide support within the learning environment.

It's important to recognize that some educators may have preconceived attitudes and understanding about spending time outdoors and what that means for learning. These can include:

> A lack of understanding about the benefits of nature-based and outdoor learning, and the perception that nature-based learning isn't important.

> A lack of knowledge about flora/fauna may lead to incorrect assumptions—for example, fear of venomous snakes or prevalence of bees, or playing in a patch of poison ivy because the adult cannot identify it.

> A dismissive attitude that children are "not learning anything" when they engage in unstructured outdoor play.

> A lack of confidence regarding how to facilitate nature-based experiences, especially outdoors.

> The fear of losing control over a group of students in an outdoor environment and children running off on their own.

> Personal phobias about animals or ecophobia (a fear of nature).

> Cultural traditions or practices that affect their perception of nature-based learning.

> Concern about providing for children with disabilities in an outdoor and unstructured environment.

> Concern about parent expectations of nature-based learning ("I told you not to get your clothes dirty!" or "Bugs are gross, don't touch that!")

Addressing these attitudes, fears, and misconceptions begins with understanding what it means and what is required to be a nature-based educator. This chapter discusses both educator and administrator roles and responsibilities in nature-based learning and nature-based education programs.

Guiding Questions

As you read through this chapter, consider the following questions:

- What are some ways teachers can establish a supportive and friendly atmosphere among the children? Among staff?

- How does a personal nature connection help teachers prepare for nature-based education?

- How can program administrators support educators to build a successful nature-based learning program?

- How are nature-based educator requirements different from those in a traditional program?

- How does the role of the teacher in nature-based learning differ from what you may expect in a traditional classroom?

Teachers provide support as children learn practical life skills, as seen here while working in the garden.

CREDIT: HUMMINGBIRD HILL NATURE LEARNING COLLECTIVE, REISTERSTOWN, MARYLAND.

Educators Create Strong Roots

A taproot provides a stronghold for growth, nestled firmly in the earth, to sustain a rapidly growing plant such as a sunflower or milkweed. The taproot upholds the plant as it absorbs nutrients from the soil and rain and takes in sunshine to grow. Without a strong, nourished taproot, the plant will not flourish, nor will it be able to withstand all the changes that are part of its journey. In early childhood education, educators ensure the right elements are available, such as sun, soil, and rain, to ensure children grow strong taproots to sustain the journey ahead. No educator can fulfill the needs of a child unless their own taproot is strong and well nourished.

Nature-based educators need great care and attention to thrive in their own right. In a literal sense, educators need specialized training and equitable pay, as well as outdoor gear and teaching materials to carry out their work. Like all educators, nature-based educators also need a positive work atmosphere where they are appreciated and empowered. They need time, space, and permission to be flexible and creative in their approaches to teaching, and to become more proficient in their own abilities. When educators are supported in this way and firmly rooted in their vision, they are better prepared to facilitate meaningful nature-based learning that is aligned with the program's goals. To that end, program administrators should consider specific ways to nurture teachers in nature-based programs.

Who doesn't love a puppet? Playful engagement is a fun way to introduce nature-based concepts.

CREDIT: PRAIRIEWOOD FOREST SCHOOL AT ST. FRANCIS OF THE WOODS, COYLE, OKLAHOMA.

Changing Perceptions

A study conducted by Julia Torquati and colleagues (2013) on the perceptions of nature-based education by educators concluded that educators were uncomfortable and less confident in implementing a nature-based curriculum when compared with other curricular domains. The researchers developed considerations for what educators need to know and understand to be effective "nature educators" (Torquati et al. 2013). Here is a summary of the five ideas discussed in the study:

1. *Having experiences in nature.* Teachers with limited experience in nature are not as likely to want to engage in outdoor learning. The more experiences teachers have in nature, the better their comfort level will be outside, which will ultimately increase their likelihood to facilitate nature-based learning.

2. *Not being afraid of nature.* Fear of nature, whether it is justified or not, will prevent teachers from taking their learning outside. Teachers need enough exposure to nature to quell any fears. Addressing these fears about plants and animals or other potential hazards will help equip teachers to take their learning outside.

3. *Knowledge of basic concepts and facts about nature.* Teachers do not need to know the names and natural history of everything living outside. Curiosity about nature is wonderful, but there is no need to be a walking field guide. In fact, it is better for children and teachers to wonder together! Being able to say "I don't know, but what can we learn by looking more closely? What do you notice?" can be the start of rich inquiry. As long as teachers know enough about the outdoor space to identify hazards on-site, any other knowledge will be attained organically, together.

4. *Having effective teaching strategies.* Learning outside is new for many teachers, and the strategies used to facilitate outdoor learning differ from indoor classroom approaches. Kids are not seated at tables! New strategies can make teachers feel anxious and insecure about implementing the curriculum. It is crucial that teachers have professional development around nature-based learning. It can also be helpful to work with a mentor or co-teacher to learn together and to observe other models that successfully implement nature-based education.

5. *Having a love of nature or excitement about the outdoors.* When teachers are enthusiastic and eager about nature-based learning, they are more likely to hone their practices to become highly effective nature-based teachers. Teachers who love nature are more likely to be encouraging and upbeat among children and colleagues alike.

Experience and Qualifications

Naturally, the expectations of nature-based educators—especially those engaging in daily outdoor learning—are different from expectations in traditional settings. Nature-based educators have a dual responsibility to combine developmentally appropriate practices in early childhood education with concepts of environmental literacy that requires educators to consider potential environmental impacts of their decisions and those of their program leadership. Not only do nature-based educators need to understand child growth and development, but they also have to work within the context of nature and the environment. For example, teachers will need to:

› Facilitate outdoor learning and interactions with nature and natural materials
› Nurture social, emotional, and cognitive connections with the land, its resources, and local natural history
› Embody environmentally conscious attitudes and behaviors

Table 4.1 Comparison of Qualifications for Nature-Based Early Childhood Educators

Essential Knowledge and/or Qualifications of Early Childhood Educators*	*Additional Recommended Experience and/or Qualifications for Nature-Based Educators*
Coursework or degree in early childhood education	Experience and/or professional training in nature-based early childhood education (e.g., undergraduate/graduate coursework in nature-based early childhood education, nature-based teacher certification, Cedarsong Way Teacher Training, or Forest School training)
	Risk management practices for outdoor nature-based programs
Pediatric first aid and CPR	Wilderness first aid and CPR or wilderness first responder, depending on the outdoor setting
Ongoing professional development in early childhood education topics such as relationships, curriculum, teaching, assessment, health, safety, community, communication with families, learning environments, professionalism, administration, and developmentally appropriate practices for relevant age groups	Experience and/or professional development in earth skills, wilderness survival, foraging, common plant and animal identification, outdoor interpretation, natural play spaces, or climate change (e.g., master naturalist or master gardener, trained beekeeper, National Outdoor Leadership School certification, Coyote Mentoring, shinrin-yoku forest bathing, training in relevant tool use)
Additional focus on inclusion and special education topics, multicultural and BIPOC perspectives, LGBTQ+ topics, anti-bias and anti-racist training, and trauma-informed care	Experience and/or professional development with or about local Indigenous groups; training that specifies inclusion strategies and accommodations for children in outdoor settings; knowledge about nature-based occupational and mental health therapies and eco-anxiety, defined as "a chronic fear of environmental doom" (Usher & Usher 2022)

*Requirements for licensed or certified early childhood educators vary from state to state and country to country.

> Help children develop an understanding of their role as part of the natural world and the impact they can have on the environment

> Safeguard children from hazards that may be present in outdoor learning environments

It's helpful to think about what all early childhood educators do and the experiences they share and then consider what is needed to be able to teach using nature pedagogy and to become a nature-based educator. Table 4.1 describes describes essential experience and qualifications that any high-quality early childhood educator or childcare provider may already have (left-hand column). The right-hand column describes additional experience useful to supporting the goals of nature-based education.

Effective Teaching Starts with Nature Connection

Is it possible to be a nature-based educator without personal nature connection? No. In terms of implementing nature-based curriculum, what teachers do is closely linked with their attitudes about nature. Teachers must be committed to their own authentic nature connection to fully realize nature-based learning with children. There is no faking it. The positive outcomes of teachers cultivating their own personal nature connection is that they become more confident and effective as their comfort in outdoor settings improves. Indeed, they look forward to their time sharing nature with the children they teach.

These teachers will also deepen relationships with the land and community because nature-based educators are responsible for nurturing place-based connections with the land in authentic ways. These nature connections can be described as:

Outdoor classrooms like this one afford opportunities for nature connection among children and their teachers.

CREDIT: MONTESSORI LUNA BILINGUAL MICRO SCHOOL, PIKESVILLE, MARYLAND.

> Meaningful engagement with nature through direct, sensory-rich experiences

> Emotional affinity for nature, which includes sense of belonging, appreciation, responsibility, empathy, and respect

> Cognitive awareness about nature, which includes identifying, observing, and naming things in nature

> Understanding of one's interconnected role as part of the natural world

Like facets on a crystal, there are many dimensions that make up our personal nature connection. Some teachers may fear or experience anxiety about being outdoors. Others may crave the creature comforts of being inside. We live in an increasingly "containerized" world, moving from one air-conditioned space to the next, which means many people feel a total disconnect (and disregard) for the role that this connection has on learning. This is to say that nature connection is not the same for everyone, and not all teachers have had positive experiences in nature. Some communities experience barriers to a nature connection due to limited access to green spaces, pervasive crime, pollution or poor air quality, or trauma that stems from climate change (e.g., devastating floods, storms, or fires). Issues such as safe, equitable access urgently demand our attention. When these barriers exist for teachers, they may also extend to the children and families in their communities. It is important to recognize that a nature connection is a unique relationship based on a range of cultural, social, and personal experiences. We must meet people where they are with sensitivity and a nonjudgmental attitude. Despite the challenges, nature-based educators will be more confident and effective as their comfort in outdoor settings improves.

The following list offers ways to inspire an authentic, place-based connection with nature:

10 Ways for Teachers to Nurture Nature Connection

1. Go outside every day, if only for a 10-minute walk.
2. Go outside in all kinds of weather. Borrow or invest in gear that allows you to be in nature in every season.
3. Grow something. Make a commitment to care for a plant for at least one growing season.
4. Learn about common trees and plants in your area. Is there one tree or plant you walk by every day that you cannot identify? Learn more about it, then begin to build your repertoire of local plant knowledge, plant by plant.
5. List five animals you regularly see outdoors (not including pets). Take time to observe their habitats and interactions outdoors. Where do they find shelter? Food? Raise their young? What natural resources do they rely on?
6. Learn more about where your waste goes. Specifically, where does the garbage truck take your trash and recyclables? Your yard waste? How are your actions impacting the local environment, and what steps can you take to minimize any negative impacts?
7. Who are the Indigenous tribes or First Nations people where you live? Research their cultural history and land-based issues that may still exist. How does this information better prepare you to interact with the land? To teach about its natural history? Become a better ally?
8. What is the nearest creek to your home? School? What body of water does it flow into? How did it get its name?
9. Make time each month to explore natural settings such as parks, sanctuaries, or nature preserves to experience and observe a variety of local ecosystems.
10. Walk around and explore your school grounds with fresh eyes. Identify spaces that have potential for outdoor learning or areas for plantings or wildlife support such as bird feeders.

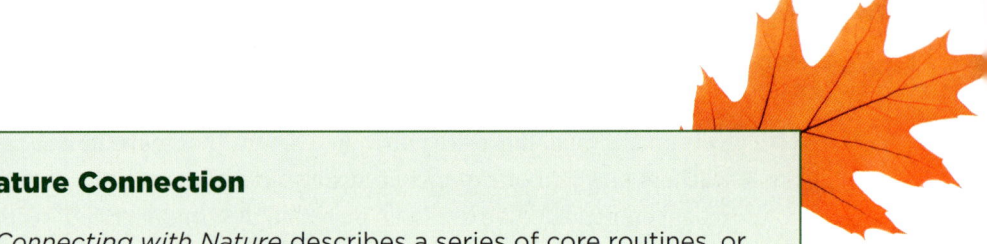

Core Routines of Nature Connection

The Coyote's Guide to Connecting with Nature describes a series of core routines, or in the authors' words, "things people do to learn nature's ways" (Young et al. 2010). These universal habits have been practiced by people for thousands of years and passed down through oral tradition. Many of us instinctively practice core routines because they are deeply ingrained habits that help people survive. When teachers facilitate core routines, they draw closer to nature and continue to pass on these essential practices to children.

Overview of Core Routines

In the following list, we introduce several core routines in brief, but if you want to learn more, there are detailed descriptions of each universal practice in *The Coyote's Guide to Connecting with Nature*. We are grateful for the awareness that these routines can instill in both teachers and children.

> **Sit Spot:** A practice of visiting the same place to know it more deeply. This practice involves sitting still and being present in the same location to develop sensory awareness and sense of place.

> **Storytelling:** Telling stories allows us to voice a collective understanding of shared experiences, which is often greater than any one individual perspective.

> **Expanding Our Senses:** We can exercise our senses to experience nature more completely.

> **Questioning and Tracking:** When we sit with questions and keep asking new ones, inquiry can reveal complicated relationships between plants, animals, and other natural phenomena. Nature is full of clues and tracks, but don't rush to offer information about them or you'll squash the child-directed inquiry that results from being curious.

> **Animal Forms:** Imitating animals is a playful way to tap into bodily learning and play out physical and behavioral adaptations. Imaginative animal play can also inspire empathy and compassion for living things.

> **Wandering:** Unstructured time for outdoor play and exploration helps us slow down and let go of the pressure of schedules. Timelessness is our gift when we plan to go off the plan.

> **Mapping:** Orienting to the natural environment is an ongoing process. We can develop a greater appreciation for the movement of the sun and the four directions of a compass as they relate to navigating time and space.

> **Exploring Field Guides:** Through oral tradition, elders have historically passed down knowledge about food sources, medicine, poisonous and venomous creatures, and so on. Today, field guides and apps now possess condensed versions of this vital information, so it is helpful to examine field guides. Always keep them handy, and empower children to find their own answers when a question arises.

> **Journaling:** Documenting our experiences on the land can offer rich accounts of seasonal changes over time. This routine provides ready-made opportunities for observation and reflection.

> **Survival Living:** Earth skills such as building shelters, making fire, and foraging activate our instincts to live on and with the land.

> **Mind's-Eye Imagining:** Cameras can capture images instantly, but careful, accurate observation is a skill that is honed over time. The practice of recalling details in one's mind can help us remember intricate details, shapes, patterns, and features found in nature, which helps shape our naturalist intelligence.

> **Listening for Bird Language:** Learning to listen to birds helps us appreciate the dynamic ways animals communicate and the impact our presence can have on other living things.

> **Thanksgiving:** We acknowledge the tremendous gifts we receive from nature, from the ground we stand on to the air we breathe. Gratitude practice reminds us of the intricate ways in which we rely on the natural world to sustain us. We give thanks for the incomparable bounty of nature and unite in reciprocity and thankfulness.

Administrators create policies that welcome outdoor exploration and ensure that both teachers and children are prepared.

These are not intended to be done in one fell swoop! Teachers can buddy up to work on this list throughout the year. Administrators can create a culture of nature-based learning by encouraging these experiences, participating alongside staff, modeling practices during reserved meeting time and professional development sessions, and implementing policies that remove barriers to learning outdoors.

How Administrators Support Educators

As seen earlier in a table, nature-based educators require additional knowledge and experience, and bear additional responsibility. The success of any early childhood program therefore depends on the commitment of the administrators to engage with and support its educators. There are key and foundational principles that, when put into practice, strengthen a program's work and benefit all children. Here are seven approaches to supporting educators when creating a new program or adapting an existing one.

1. Sharing the Program's Vision for a Nature-Based Curriculum

When educators engage in shaping not only the mission but also a shared vision for the future, they become more unified in purpose and in practice. More than a mission statement, a program's vision encompasses values and hope for the future. It is the "why" of what you do embodied in a dream that you work toward every day. Vision statements declare an ideal and a statement of hope (Carter et al. 2020). It includes aspirations to support all children and nurture the next generation of stewards. To succeed, a program's vision cannot belong to one person alone. Whether creating a nature-based program from the beginning or bringing nature-based learning to your program, educators must be engaged in the process and committed to the mission. If an educator does not have proclivity for nature or the environment, it will be difficult for them to adapt.

2. Orientation and Preparation of Nature-Based Educators

A comprehensive orientation for educators helps flesh out how they facilitate the daily rhythm; curriculum and assessment; safety practices; behavior management; interactions with colleagues; communication with parents; environmental ethos; commitment to diversity, equity, and inclusion; and other relevant professional standards. While no educator can be expected to memorize everything on day one, having a thorough orientation provides a clear framework and access to resources that are a trail map for greater success.

3. Committing to Nature

Educators need supportive administrators who model a commitment to earth-friendly, sustainable practices that demonstrate how the program "walks the walk." Administrators must understand the needs of educators to create and sustain an authentic nature-based program and provide funding and support. Administrators should routinely spend time in the outdoor learning environment alongside educators, children, and families as part of the culture in any nature-based school or program.

4. Collaborating as a Team

Just as teachers meet children where they are, developmentally speaking, teachers are also on individualized journeys. Ongoing team building activities can help teaching staff gel and can be scaffolded into weekly team meetings, after-class debriefs, or lesson-planning meetings.

Mentorship is a highly effective way to form supportive professional relationships among your team, especially when implemented as a mentorship over the course of a school year. Seasoned teachers may be mentors to newer teachers, taking them under their wings, so to speak. Less formal than a mentorship, teachers may shadow one another's classes within the same program to compare practices and learn from each other. In some instances, teachers visit other similar nature-based programs in the community. This allows teachers to learn from one another in a spirit of building capacity for high-quality nature-based education rather than viewing similar programs as competition.

It is important to establish an atmosphere of learning and growth as a team in support of carrying out a shared vision. A nonjudgmental growth mindset is helpful among colleagues to build a foundation of trust and cooperation. Program staff should remain open to new ideas, acknowledge skills, and hone the strengths of everyone on the team. This creates a reflective culture where everyone is valued and encouraged to share fresh perspectives. Once an emergent curriculum is underway, open discussion and collaboration is paramount. Teachers must be able to come together, one in purpose, to support children's development.

5. Engaging in Ongoing Professional Development

Teachers spend time in nature during the weeklong Nature-Based Teacher Certification course presented by the Association for Nature-Based Education. It is also offered as a six-week virtual course, which still includes networking and skills-based practices.

CREDIT: ASSOCIATION FOR NATURE-BASED EDUCATION.

Atiya Wells, founding director of Backyard Basecamp, offers a tour of BLISS Meadows during a professional development course in Baltimore, Maryland.

CREDIT: ASSOCIATION FOR NATURE-BASED EDUCATION.

There are a range of topics educators and administrators can explore in professional development, but as every professional knows, new learning from professional development can be fleeting. To make the most of professional development courses, educators should have opportunities to reflect on new learning, share important ideas with fellow staff (or, in some cases, parents), and apply newly learned approaches that support program goals. As an extension of professional development, educators should have opportunities to network with colleagues, visit other programs, conduct research, contribute to publications, make presentations, and advocate for nature-based early childhood education.

In terms of large conferences for nature-based professionals, the Natural Start Alliance and the Children & Nature Network both offer annual, multiday conferences with scores of seminars and workshops to choose from. These conferences typically feature an expert keynote, plenary, and research poster sessions for a well-rounded selection of topics in outdoor, nature-based, and environmental education. For smaller, more localized training, the Association for Nature-Based Education (ANBE) offers Outdoor Teacher Retreats that rotate to different cities, sowing seeds of inspiring practices and fostering connection among educators that help nature-based programs grow at the local level. ANBE's Nature-Based Teacher Certification and other similar forest and nature school training programs offer in-depth training over several weeks or months, which provides a supportive community of practice to prepare educators and administrators for working with children in a range of nature-based settings. Topics include nature-based pedagogy and curriculum, health and safety considerations (i.e., outdoor toileting, exploring bodies of water, playing with sticks), emergency planning, how to identify local plants/animals, documentation and assessment, and approaches to diversity, equity, and inclusion in nature-based early childhood education, just to name a few. Not least of all, these programs provide hands-on skills practice that are unique to outdoor, nature-based programs. If you are seeking a degreed certificate program in nature-based education at an institution for higher learning, Antioch University in New Hampshire and Prescott College in Arizona are two excellent starting points.

Meaningful professional development goes beyond learning one skill or activity, or an afternoon of policy updates. In the fullest sense, professional development has the power to be transformative.

Longtime naturalist and educator Julie Biedrzycki shares foraging practices during hands-on professional development.

CREDIT: JESSICA LEWIS.

A beautiful tea station beckons teachers during a forest bathing workshop.

CREDIT: KATIE ROONEY.

Invitations to play aren't just for children! Teachers are inspired by this nature art invitation during a Nature-Based Teacher Certification course at Lime Hollow Nature Center in Cortland, New York.

CREDIT: ASSOCIATION FOR NATURE-BASED EDUCATION.

It should supply educators with an ever-widening repertoire of professional experiences and networks that support them along their nature-based paths. While these programs are focused on professional growth for educators, there is no denying that a commitment to personal growth—especially regarding self-care, social and emotional intelligence, and nature connection—all develop traits that are necessary to be an effective nature-based educator.

6. Supporting Teacher Self-Care Through Nature Connection

Administrators must support the mental and physical well-being of the educators in their program. In nature-based education, allowing time to foster nature connection, as described earlier, not only improves educators' familiarity and comfort teaching outside but is also therapeutic and promotes all kinds of health and stress-relieving benefits for adults—not only children! Some of these include physical activity and exercise, lower heart rate, and feelings of calm and balance (Barrable et al. 2024; Harvard Health Publishing 2020). In this light, nature connection can also be an important part of teachers' self-care.

7. Promoting Reflective Teaching Practices

Nature-based educators must be committed to their own growth, and administrators must support ways for educators to reflect and evaluate. In-depth, personal reflection is sometimes referred to as "inner tracking." To use a nature metaphor, it's like tracking an animal to understand its behavior; inner tracking refers to the questions we ask ourselves to better understand our actions. Inner tracking is a highly individualized form of reflection that examines each educator's inner dialogue and backstory to support continuous growth.

Inner tracking dovetails with reflective teaching practices. Ongoing reflection helps us analyze our interactions with a similar growth mindset. Reflection topics may include:

> Interactions with children
> Interactions with staff
> Interactions with families
> Interactions with the learning environment, outdoor spaces, or natural settings
> Understanding/implementation of policies, procedures, or safety guidelines
> Understanding/implementation of curriculum, documentation, and assessment
> Use of tools or materials
> Child development, milestones, and developmentally appropriate practices
> Support for children with diverse abilities or needs
> School culture, earth-friendly habits, and community-building
> Personal preparedness to teach in outdoor environments and an understanding of local natural history

A collection of baskets beckons teachers to gather natural materials during a professional development session. Delightful baskets were shared courtesy of nature-based educator and mentor Amy Beam.

CREDIT: ASSOCIATION FOR NATURE-BASED EDUCATION.

As teachers strive to help children grow and follow their interests, it is natural to reflect on the interactions, activities, and experiences that are put into practice each day. Following time with children, it's important for teachers to have time to debrief the day's experiences. This serves as a way to co-create curriculum and helps teachers develop a daily practice of reflection to enhance learning. The following "Self-Reflection for Teachers" is shared with permission from the Association for Nature-Based Education. It provides a range of questions that teachers can consider each day or explore as a team during weekly meetings.

NOTE: *Topics for professional development will arise through ongoing reflection, both independently and as a staff.*

SELF-REFLECTION FOR TEACHERS

Use these questions to consider your interactions following class each day. You may want to share your reflections with a co-teacher, during a team meeting, or as a way to track your growth. The purpose of this refleciton is to note how our attitudes and actions impact the learning community and find ways to grow in a positive spirit for the benefit of all.

Children	How did I demonstrate genuine care and concern for a child(ren) today? Describe how you noticed a child(ren) express compassion today and reflect on what your response/reaction was to it. How did I express empathy and/or model taking the perspective of a child today? In what ways did I model attitudes of gratitude, kindness, and/or forgiveness to children? In what ways did I experience receiving them? How did I model (or observe) perseverance and determination to accomplish something or take a risk? Was there a child(ren) who needed extra help or support today? How did I provide that support? How might I improve support I provide tomorrow? I demonstrated calm or patience with a child today when …
Nature/ Natural Learning Environment	How did I model a positive attitude and enthusiasm towards being outdoors? What specific way(s) did I model caretaking for the land and/or spaces in the learning environment? What is one new plant, animal, or aspect of nature that I discovered today? I demonstrated calm and/or patience with the environment when …

© 2024 ASSOCIATION FOR NATURE-BASED EDUCATION | ANBE.ORG

SELF-REFLECTION FOR TEACHERS

Families	How was I present and available to parents/caregivers who wanted to talk about their child? How did I make myself available to parents/caregivers who are not physically present for drop-off/pick up or those who seem distant or hesitant to talk/communicate about their child? In what ways did I offer positive feedback about a child(ren) today to a family? What did I do, specifically, to help make learning visible for families? I demonstrated calm and/or patience with a parent/caregiver when … What differences did I notice that need further consideration regarding someone's culture, background, or abilities? In what ways can I address them to better support the child/family?
Co-workers and Staff	In what ways did I provide support to my colleague(s) today? What did I notice a colleague do today that felt inspiring or significant? In what ways did I demonstrate flexibility today? What specific ways did I observe a colleague demonstrating flexibility? How did I model positivity and trustworthiness to my colleague(s) today? I demonstrated calm and/or patience with a colleague(s) when … Describe the most significant way you worked with a colleague to implement a safety routine(s) today.

OTHER REFLECTIONS ABOUT TODAY:

Opportunities for nature connection can also provide calming space for reflection. This teacher examines milkweed during a visit to the nature preschool at Irvine Nature Center in Owings Mills, Maryland.

CREDIT: ASSOCIATION FOR NATURE-BASED EDUCATION.

The ideas offered in this chapter highlight what both educators and administrators can do to ensure that nature-based learning flourishes and children thrive. While there are many emergent learning opportunities that arise in nature-based programs, it takes an intentional, ongoing commitment to nature-based practices to make the most of those moments. As you grow as a nature-based educator, many of these practices will become engrained both professionally as well as personally. To be authentic as a nature-based educator, you will deepen your personal nature connection as you cultivate ways to facilitate nature-based learning and play.

Reflection Questions

> What additional training and/or skills are important for nature-based educators?

> How might you go about deepening your authentic connection to nature?

> Review the schedule for a typical child's day in your program. What percentage is fully child directed? How much (nonrecess) time is spent outdoors engaged in learning and play?

> Consider the role of inner tracking (personal reflection) and reflective teaching practices (professional reflection) on your work with young children. How do these approaches support a growth mindset approach for nature-based educators?

CALL TO ACTION

Create your own Reflective Practices Journal, then identify one question from the Self-Reflection for Teachers document and respond to it as your first journal entry.

CHAPTER 5

Visioning and Managing a Nature-Based Program

The practices shared in previous chapters are the most effective when they are implemented as part of an overarching vision to guide your program. Without a framework that gives context to nature-based practices, even the best intentions can fall short. This chapter will help you explore key ideas to craft a cohesive, thoughtful vision that supports nature-based learning in your program.

Guiding Questions

As you read through this chapter, consider the following questions:

- How can nature-based programs support children and families?

- What does an inclusive nature-based program look like?

- What practical responsibilities do educators and administrators have in a nature-based learning program?

- How does an administrator's role differ in a nature-based program? As you read, note items you may need to review in light of establishing nature-based practices.

Trail Map for Planning a Nature-Based Program

Whether you are creating a new program or want to increase nature-based learning at an existing school, start by reflecting on program basics. What vision is at the heart of your program, and how do your policies and practices support this vision? These are weighty questions that involve research, collaboration, and ongoing consideration, so pace yourself! If you are planning with a group (i.e., staff, advisory board, families), allow plenty of time to fully examine each question. This isn't something intended to be completed in one sitting.

There is no one-size-fits-all formula to get the perfect blend. Each program must determine what works best based on the vision, goals, and needs of the learning community. A reflective process among administrators, educators, families, and children can help inform what the right balance is. The following questions can help you get started. (Visit or click on https://www.naeyc.org/resources/pubs/nature-based-ece to download a tool to help you organize your answers.)

Foundational Program Components

> What is the mission and vision of your program?

> What is your educational philosophy? How do you believe children learn best?

> How do assessment methods support your vision and educational philosophy?

> What is the rhythm of the day for children and staff? What is the amount of time classes are held indoors and outdoors each day? How are time frames determined?

> What learning environments are needed or best suited to your vision? Include thoughts on indoor and outdoor settings, as well as emergency spaces.

> Who will be able to access your program? What will you do to cultivate equitable access and a welcoming atmosphere? (For example, families with limited income, single-parent or nontraditional households, families who identify as BIPOC or LGBTQ+, multilanguage speakers, children with special medical or behavioral needs, unhoused families.)

> How will your program model values consistent with conservation, sustainability, and environmental literacy? How could community partners support your efforts?

All children benefit from outdoor, nature-based learning. Here, children are geared up in rain suits provided by the school and ready to explore.

CREDIT: FALLS CHURCH–MCLEAN CHILDREN'S CENTER.

Program Administration

> What income and expenses does your program have? What financial aid options are available to families? Do they provide adequate support? What questions do you have about liability, health, and safety practices? How will you address these questions?

> Do your educators have appropriate skills and knowledge for a nature-based program? What kind of training and credentials do teaching staff and administrators need to implement this vision?

> What will the staffing pattern look like? What hiring and staff evaluation procedures are in place? What compensation and benefits will be available for staff to ensure fair, livable wages?

Approaches to Teaching and Learning

> What skills and values do you prioritize for your learning community?

> What intentions, goals, or objectives do you have for learning?

> What is the purpose of your curriculum?

> How do the children's ideas factor into the curriculum?

> How are children nurtured based on their unique backgrounds, needs, and interests?

> How is nature-based learning part of daily practices, teaching, and learning in your program?

> How do you make the process of learning visible? What strategies are used to document learning? What forms of assessment are used?

> In what ways do educators address early learning standards?

Teachers and administrators work together to offer meaningful opportunities for nature-based learning while ensuring that children are safe.

CREDIT: MIAMI NATURE PLAYSCHOOL.

Once you have thoroughly examined these questions, you can dig into more nuanced policies and approaches to implement your vision. A business plan can serve as a template to think through the unique administrative, programmatic, curricular, financial, environmental, and contextual factors that guide your vision. You will need to determine what your policies are on topics such as foraging, playing with sticks, collecting or picking things from nature, tree climbing, protocols for gathering around a fire, and interaction with wildlife, just to name a few. Parents and guardians will also want to know how you approach handwashing, outdoor napping, and backcountry toileting as they pertain to your outdoor learning environment. Policies should be clearly articulated in your Parent/Guardian Handbook, and expectations should be reinforced with educators who are fully oriented to the program. Additional parent meetings and workshops should be held in parallel with ongoing meetings and professional development for staff throughout the school year. This establishes consistency in communication with families and staff. Note that an emergency preparedness plan is another vital document that educators must be oriented to; ongoing review of this plan is crucial for safety purposes. Emergency planning is one key feature of an educator's orientation and coincides with policies that are in your Parent/Guardian Handbook.

Honoring Children and Families

High-quality early childhood programs promote positive relationships and "encourage each child's sense of individual worth" (NAEYC 2019b). This grounding principle centers our belief in honoring children and families by building respectful relationships that embrace the whole child.

Adding to this, nature-based early childhood programs emphasize child-directed, emergent learning and a range of approaches that help children find purpose in their daily experiences. This distinct child-nature focus is embedded in nature-based pedagogy. It hinges on teachers inviting children to make connections with each other and the natural world while being supported in an enriching learning environment.

A Commitment to Every Child

Early care and education is vital for every child, so it is crucial to examine any potential barriers that families face when it comes to accessing nature-based programs. One starting point

Children take turns using a magnifying glass as they learn about seeds and seed pods.

CREDIT: MONTESSORI LUNA BILINGUAL MICRO SCHOOL, PIKESVILLE, MARYLAND.

Caretaking includes watering plants, seen here as a child pours from a watering can. Activities like this help children develop motor skills and an understanding of what different plants need to survive and thrive.

CREDIT: PRAIRIEWOOD FOREST SCHOOL AT ST. FRANCIS OF THE WOODS, COYLE, OKLAHOMA.

Unstructured nature play encourages children to socialize, develop language skills, and regulate emotions while they interact with natural materials in creative ways.

CREDIT: GOOSEBERRY NATURE SCHOOL, COVINGTON, KENTUCKY.

may be to learn about the demographics in your community, then consider who attends your program. Does the learning community reflect the makeup of your local community? Why or why not? A program assessment can help you evaluate policies and other factors that may unintentionally prevent families with significant financial challenges or People of Color from participating.

If you are opening a new nature-based program, consider the location(s) of similar programs and who they already serve. Do children from low socio-economic status currently have access to these programs? Do children from underserved communities have equitable access to nature-based programs? If not, how can your program ensure that everyone is welcome and included in an equitable way?

Connecting with other nonprofit organizations and outside consultants can help you to address any barriers to equitable learning. They can also provide an objective perspective as an onlooker learning about your program. It is difficult, if not impossible, for a program director to objectively evaluate inequitable structures and practices that are already baked into a program—no matter how unintentional the barriers may be.

A surprising point here is that licensed childcare programs in each state are tasked with providing access and support to the most vulnerable children, especially those who live in low-resourced communities and Title 1 areas. Ironically, fully immersive outdoor preschools are only legally licensed in Washington state. Maryland is currently engaged in a four-year outdoor preschool licensing pilot program, which began in 2023, while Oregon and Colorado have since enacted laws to license immersive outdoor preschools. This means that the current system of licensing in 47 of 50 U.S. states still perpetuates systemic, inequitable access to immersive outdoor learning programs. Families who rely on state vouchers, scholarships, or subsidies for childcare can only use them in licensed programs. The inability to be licensed has an unfortunate domino effect. Consider that unlicensed outdoor preschools must operate for shorter hours to legally comply with state restrictions regarding what constitutes childcare (regulations vary greatly from state to state). Tuition-based outdoor preschool programs with short, half-day hours are simply not an option for working families in need of full-time childcare. As a result of this socio-economic barrier, advocacy groups are forming across the United States to lobby for outdoor preschool licensing, thereby compelling state departments of education to develop outdoor preschool licensing standards through legislative action.

There are many emerging resources and research that examine issues of equitable access to nature-based education and related issues of environmental justice. Carolyn Finney's book *Black*

NOTE: *If you are seeking books with greater representation of diverse people and perspectives, The Brown Bookshelf: United in Story is a fantastic online resource (https://thebrownbookshelf.com).*

Faces, White Spaces: Reimagining the Relationship of African Americans to the Great Outdoors frames the conversation within a historical context (Finney 2014). Other organizations such as the Prevention Institute are tackling structural issues that impact access to parks and green spaces (Prevention Institute, n.d.). The National Association for the Education of Young Children has related resources for educators that emphasize equitable access to childcare, including their position statement, *Advancing Equity in Early Childhood Education* (NAEYC 2019a).

Helpful Strategies and Considerations for Challenges in Outdoor Learning

If exploring outdoors with young children is a new class routine, here are a few common behaviors to be aware of along with ideas of how to address each of them.

Behavior	Helpful Strategies and Considerations
Child wants to be carried or wants an adult to carry backpack or gear	Backpacks should be appropriately sized for children, and while there are some essential items to carry, be sure they are not overloaded with unnecessary items. With that accounted for, children can carry their own gear … and their own bodies! Pace the group to ensure there are hydration and snack breaks, along with frequent rest periods. Remember, it takes time to build endurance, especially for younger children or those new to outdoor learning that involves vigorous activity. Ensure that staff are spaced out to accommodate children who are ready to move and those who take more time to hike from one place to the next. (One teacher leads at the front; the other is at the back of the trail group.) Some teachers opt for a trail wagon to help carry gear such as backpacks and water bottles—with the children's help, of course!
Child runs ahead of trail group or runs away	Safety expectations set the tone for all outdoor learning. It can be dangerous or disruptive for a child to run ahead of the lead teacher or for a child to go off trail (or established outdoor classroom boundaries). Before venturing on a trail walk, be clear about who must lead the group, and talk about why. Involve children in taking a head count before moving from one place to the next. If a child inches ahead, make a point to stop and remind them to walk beside or behind the lead teacher. It can be helpful for each child to have a regular "buddy" to walk with, which also helps them account for one another during trail walks.

Behavior	Helpful Strategies and Considerations
Child wants to run versus walk	When children run, they demonstrate their need to use gross, locomotor, and proprioception skills. If you say yes to running and run with children more often, they will be less prone to sprinting at inopportune times. Pretend you are a herd of deer and run together, play a game of "squirrel tag," or run to meet at a fixed stopping point. For children that crave running, be sure to build in plenty of opportunities each day. When children run to a fixed stopping point, visual cues such as a trail sign, stone cairn, painted log, or other memorable natural features can be useful reminders of where to stop.
Aggressive behavior towards other people, property, or living things	Teachers can model appreciation and respect by thanking a favorite climbing tree or rock, mending or caring for gear, and problem solving if something gets damaged or broken. Teachers also model respect for living creatures through observation, not necessarily handling. Children develop greater kindness and perspective-taking when they have calm, gentle examples from teachers. When aggression occurs, conflict resolution can help children make amends and process the experience. Avoid overreacting to aggression, and model forgiveness so that each child can have a fresh start and move on after an upsetting incident. Plan for supportive, individualized approaches with co-teachers, administrators, parents, and the child if you observe a pattern of aggressive behavior.
Collecting or keeping plants, animals, or other elements from nature	Establish a policy around collecting, and make sure staff know how to consistently apply it. Such policies can help children develop an ethic of care, conservation, and preservation. In many cases, it is beneficial to have direct experience with small vertebrates (e.g., toads, salamanders, or fish) and invertebrates (e.g., ants, beetles, worms, or crayfish). Likewise, if children come across a tuft of fur, feathers, antlers, or scat, for example, they may want to examine it more closely. Teachers should give specific guidance before children interact with elements found in nature while fully encouraging inquiry when possible. Handwashing procedures should always be enforced.
Tasting and foraging wild edibles	Plant identification is a natural aspect of outdoor learning. It can be gratifying to find and forage wild edibles, and many are plentiful and nutritious. Be sure parents grant permission for foraging as part of your enrollment agreement. Set parameters for foraging with a teacher's permission, and never allow children to taste plants unless you can identify them with 100 percent certainty. Demonstrate how to express gratitude for the generosity of the plants, for example, by sharing a bit of water to give the plant a drink. Wild salads, berries, and teas are a few foraged favorites.
Playing with sticks	Teachers need to establish consistent policies for carrying sticks, wielding them during play, running, hitting, or building with them. For example, during a trail walk, you may want to specify the size of a stick and require one end to always touch the ground. This prevents a horizontal stick from poking a friend. Running with sticks can be dangerous, so set clear expectations and give reminders as needed.

(Continued)

Helpful Strategies and Considerations for Challenges in Outdoor Learning (*Continued*)

Behavior	Helpful Strategies and Considerations
Good guy versus bad guy play; rough-and-tumble play	Play themes of good versus bad play out repeatedly as a way for children to explore power dynamics and consequences of choices. This kind of play incorporates social skills and pretend play, which are beneficial, but can escalate into something that feels too scary for some children. The thrill of rough-and-tumble play can also be irresistible and may occur briefly, then wane, as part of a game. Children should always feel physically and emotionally safe, and discussion around consent will help empower children during social interactions that involve risky play. As a staff, teachers should determine what kinds of play warrant stepping in (e.g., "Is this a game that everyone wants to play?"). Children should learn to ask for consent and know they have a choice about whether to give it.

As evident in this list, children reveal the skills and attitudes that they want (or, more likely, need) to develop during their nature play. It is helpful to remember that when we observe challenging behavior, it is a useful insight into what areas of support children may need.

Each of these examples from the table require a great deal of self-reflection. Consider these questions:

› How do you set the tone for children to meet specific expectations?
› How do you react to the most challenging behaviors? How might you reframe them?
› Is there one child or group of children who need more support or a different approach? What strategies have been most successful?
› What resources do you still need to confidently manage repetitive, challenging behavior?
› Who can you look to as a mentor for additional guidance and support?

Beyond personal reflection, administrators and teachers must work closely to establish consistent policies and routines that consider the program's unique goals, setting, and dynamics. The best policies strike a balance between providing freedom and choice with the safety and well-being of the entire learning community. Ongoing program evaluation is crucial, especially as it relates to beneficial risky play and potential safety concerns (for more on risky play, see Chapter 3). By establishing policies that are authentic to nature-based learning, you can work through these challenges and honor children's need for safety and support.

Children with Disabilities

All children benefit from nature-based learning, and it is our duty to ensure that every child can access these benefits. Ruth Wilson, renowned researcher and author, makes several points about why children in special education programs need an integrated approach to nature-based education. Both special education and nature-based education share goals of holistic child development. Offered in unison, teachers can increase motivation to learn, provide interdisciplinary learning experiences that are appropriate for children with individualized learning needs, and cultivate environmental literacy for all students (Wilson 1994; 2022).

In her 2022 book *Naturally Inclusive: Engaging Children of All Abilities Outdoors*, Wilson underscores the role of outdoor play spaces as a context for more accessible nature-based learning and play. She notes, "A well-designed inclusive play space reduces barriers for children with special needs, creating an environment where children with differing abilities can engage in similar play behaviors with their typically developing peers" (Wilson 2022, 93). That is, inclusive outdoor play can encourage all children—with and without disabilities—to play together. Children cannot develop social skills if they don't have peers to interact with, and inclusive outdoor play spaces can help address this barrier to social and emotional development.

In some cases, educators struggle to provide accommodations for children with disabilities, or feel they lack administrative support to effectively make necessary accommodations. Yet the Americans with Disabilities Act (ADA), signed into law in 1990, is a landmark civil rights law that prohibits discrimination against people with disabilities. The Individuals with Disabilities Education Act (IDEA) dovetails with ADA and states that "free and appropriate" education and services must be available to all children (Colker 2004; Condrey & Brudney 1998; U.S. Department of Education, n.d.).

Despite these laws, some families of children with disabilities are discouraged or turned away from nature-based programs by those claiming the program "may not be the right fit." Although not legal, the reasons cited by some programs include:

- Lack of staff support if one-to-one assistance is necessary or there is no funding to provide an aide
- Lack of staff training regarding a particular physical, emotional, medical, or behavioral condition
- Concerns about site-specific outdoor features (e.g., grade/slope of terrain, nearby body of water, transportation to or from outdoor location, or other hazards)
- Desire to accommodate the majority of typically developing children; inflexibility regarding making accommodations for children with special needs
- Concerns from parents or staff regarding the impact of inclusion
- Lack of resources for families requiring special education and support services
- Feeling that a child with special needs may be better served some place else that already has accommodations in place
- Lack of funding to address any or all these challenges

If these barriers exist in your nature-based program, it is time to become a fierce advocate for inclusive solutions! Often the entire learning community will benefit from parent education and professional development around inclusion and working with children with physical and developmental disabilities. There is plenty of research and resources that demonstrate the benefits of nature-based education for *all* children. When the learning community becomes informed of the many challenges faced by children with disabilities, they are more likely to rally behind you to determine and implement equitable solutions.

Each state can provide resources through their office of child care or department of youth and family services, and more locally at the parish or county level (the names of these departments vary from state to state). There are many nonprofit organizations that provide free resources for families and training for teachers that you can locate through some sleuthing online. If your learning community includes staff and/or volunteers with disabilities, they may have important insights to help navigate some of these barriers as well.

Knowing Your Options

When it comes to addressing the financial realities of removing barriers (e.g., the need for a one-on-one aide), the first step is to commit to ensuring inclusive access to your program. Once you've decided everyone is welcome and included, you can cast your net to find resources and support that are specific to your learning community. It may take dedication and hard work (sad, but true), but if you make your commitment to inclusion known, and share challenges you are up against, others will rise to the occasion to help. Reach out to form partnerships with those who can help, such as local and state organizations, businesses, and families in your community. You will be heartened by all the ways people will help you ensure inclusive access to the enriching nature-based learning opportunities in your program.

Seasoned special educators from the Seattle Children's PlayGarden published an insightful curricular resource in 2021 for inclusive nature-based programs. The authors assert, "Nature based preschools, like many private schools, routinely deny access to children with developmental, physical, or medical differences" (Bullard et al. 2021, 8). They urge nature-based educators to "teach our community to expect inclusion" (Bullard et al. 2021, 9). They challenge the stigma of inclusion, stating:

> You may think that fully including children with disabilities is too hard, too expensive, too risky or too much work. You may think you don't have the training, enough staff or the right equipment. You may think that there are "special" programs for "those kids" so you don't need to accept them. You may think that including a child with a disability will slow the "regular" kids down. You may feel unprepared, insecure or scared and perhaps, most commonly, you may not think about kids with disabilities at all. (Bullard et al. 2021, 8)

Bullard and her colleagues highlight the challenges that many children with special needs face, and they underscore our duty to honor them with inclusive policies that ensure equitable access to nature-based programs. Clearly, barriers to inclusion persist.

Children with disabilities often stand to receive the greatest developmental benefits as a result of participating in nature-based programs. It is every child's right to receive accommodations, not only as a legal obligation but also as a moral obligation. If we strive to help children understand the interconnectedness and diversity found in the natural world, then we must also honor and celebrate diversity among our learning communities.

Cultivating Trust and Respect with Families

Trust begins with respect for all children, their needs, backgrounds, abilities, and ideas. Long before meeting new students, teachers establish trust and respect in their communication with families. This may happen in several ways:

> **Web, social media presence, and marketing materials:** By utilizing these tools, families can become familiar with your mission and goals, as well as your expectations and enrollment options. Families will see photos and videos of children in action, which will give them a glimpse of the program, and they can seek out online reviews and recommendations. In addition, a diverse representation of your program attendees will help families feel welcome.

> **Parent/guardian/family handbook:** Clearly defined policies and procedures for a range of topics—from toileting and gear to sibling discounts and financial assistance—will establish expectations and better prepare families.

> **Program visits and tours:** Providing families with the opportunity to meet administrators and teachers will offer them a chance to observe classes and ask candid questions about what to expect.

> **Parent testimonials:** Connecting families with those who are currently enrolled provides insight into the parents' experience.

> **Word of mouth:** Families will ask around to learn about your program and hear other parents' positive experiences when deciding to enroll. Your reputation in the community is arguably the best way to build lasting trust.

For these reasons, it is crucial that the outward-facing elements of your program (e.g., website or social media) truthfully depict how learning takes place. Upon enrollment, open communication should continue; when parents ask questions, they should receive prompt, thorough answers from administrators and teachers. Though many questions can often be answered online or in your handbook, that won't replace a parent's need to develop trust with people who lead the program. With each communication, trusting parent and guardian relationships will grow. These interactions build trust leading up to drop-off on day 1 (and beyond).

For children, the process of building trust and establishing respect is on a different trajectory because they have limited opportunities to get to know teachers before starting class. Here are a few ways to build trust with children leading up to the start of a new school year:

> **Take a hike:** Invite families to spend time on the grounds so children can become familiar with the land and its special places. Provide an opportunity to practice outdoor toileting if that is part of the program.

Parents rely on teachers to implement safety practices that are specific to outdoor nature-based programs, especially around potential hazards such as fire and water. This child learns to strike a match to start a campfire with adult guidance; in this case, the child's parent is also the teacher.

CREDIT: DISCOVERY WILDERNESS SCHOOL, GRAND RAPIDS, MICHIGAN.

Caring for animals is a feature of many nature-based programs. In some cases, these programs are referred to as "farm and forest schools."

CREDIT: CLASSEN MONTESSORI SCHOOL, NORMAN, OKLAHOMA.

> **Home visit:** Arrange for teachers to visit the child at their home, and have them bring a special gift along to offer a token of kindness and add excitement for the start of school (e.g., a magnifying glass). Home visits provide important insight into children and their families.

> **Letter to the child from the teacher(s):** Include a photo of each teacher, a few of their interests, and some questions for the children. It may also include an outdoor activity or foraging recipe that teachers will reference when school begins.

> **Video greeting:** Teachers can provide a virtual tour of the outdoor classroom, share the class welcome song, and extend a warm hello. Teachers may opt to show what's in their backpack, useful gear, or other learning materials that they are excited to use when class gets started.

> **Nature playdates:** Offer an informal way for families to meet; this is a nice icebreaker for everyone—teachers, parents, and children.

> **"Getting to know you" questionnaire:** Parents can ask children to respond to each question and record their responses. This questionnaire gives teachers a better understanding of their families, traditions, and interests.

> **Orientation day:** Children get a firsthand look at their learning environment, indoors and outside. They meet teachers and peers and do a scavenger hunt to get acquainted with where things are (don't forget to include the toilet!). This is a "no pressure" kind of experience that helps children dip their toes in the water before a drop-off class.

When we take time to thoughtfully prepare welcoming experiences such as these, we acknowledge that children need time and space to build trust with teachers and peers in a new learning environment. This is especially important for children as they get to know a new outdoor setting and encounter new expectations. Children with previous experience in formal or traditional programs will also need time to adjust to the different expectations. Each of these are important opportunities to demonstrate kindness, offer accommodations, and express a sincere interest in getting to know each child while establishing trust. (See the sample "Getting to Know You Questionnaire" in the appendix at the end of this chapter.)

Showing love and respect for each child's family is another way we honor children. Families come in all kinds, and there is no such thing as a "normal" family! Children may be raised by one, both, or neither of their parents—biological, stepparents, adopted, or otherwise. Children may have parents in the LGBTQ+ community or may be raised by grandparents, older siblings, or other extended family members. Children may be recent immigrants, refugees, or move frequently with a family member who is in the armed services. The child may be under the care of social services, living with a foster family, or experiencing homelessness. Every child's home life impacts their growth and development. When we show love, care, and support not only for children but also for their families, we honor who they are.

NOTE: *The acronym LGBTQ+ represents "lesbian, gay, bisexual, transgender and queer" with a "+" sign to recognize the limitless sexual orientations and gender identities used by members of the community (Human Rights Campaign 2023).*

Planning for the Day-to-Day

There are many tasks to carry out each day that look different from a traditional classroom, and they are largely dependent on the nature-based setting where you teach. For example, in an immersive outdoor forest preschool, educators must set up handwashing stations daily if there is no running water in the immediate outdoor classroom(s) and ensure adequate potable drinking water is on site at all times. Children typically bring their own filled water bottle to school each day but may need to refill it. If a child comes without their bottle, drinking water must still be readily available.

In addition to doing a daily site scan to check for hazards each day, educators will need to ensure that they have materials and activities that are appropriate for the day's weather conditions. There are many factors to consider. If it is a cold day and children are wearing mittens, emphasis will not be on fine motor activities but instead may include running games or other activities with active gross motor play. If rain is in the forecast, educators should hang tarps for rain shelter or plan to meet in covered spaces and consider how to incorporate rainwater and mud activities for the day (mud kitchen, anyone?). On windy days, clipboards may be needed to hold nature journals open, or stones may be used to secure materials that can blow away. On especially hot days, ice and water play or stream exploration can help keep children cool. Because weather conditions are constantly changing, administrators and educators keep an eye on the weather forecast daily and send out extra reminders to families about how to dress appropriately for the weather. Likewise, remind parents about insect repellent and sunscreen regularly to ensure parents prepare their children for outdoor conditions. Policies vary from state to state concerning if, when, or how educators may apply things like tick repellent or sunscreen to children. Be sure to clearly communicate these policies to families and staff.

The care and storage of materials is another important aspect of outdoor nature-based learning. For ease of setup and breakdown, it is helpful to have storage benches, cabinets, or a shed to house materials and extra gear. Hand trowels, shovels, and other tools are more prone to breakage and rust if left out in the elements and can present tripping hazards if they get buried under leaf litter. It's important that children learn to participate in cleaning up of shared materials, just as they would indoors! Pots and pans in the mud kitchen should be stowed in a cabinet or turned upside down when not in use to prevent rainwater from accumulating (which can attract mosquitoes). This also ensures that standing water is never present as a drowning hazard, especially if families play when staff are not present. Logs and tree stumps are frequently incorporated into outdoor classrooms and naturally decay with time, and depending on the use of the logs, you may need to relocate ones that begin to rot and replace them with more freshly sourced wood. But there is also a great deal of learning that comes with the process of decomposition as children notice fungi and insects that join the process.

NOTE: *Outdoor nature-based programs avoid the use of plastics and opt for more sustainable wood and metal supplies when possible to avoid the throwaway mindset of disposable, less durable plastic goods. When plastic items get broken and tossed, this contributes to trash in landfills. Furthermore, when plastics break down in the soil, they create toxic microplastics that are harmful to the environment.*

Immersive outdoor programs use natural materials to create an inviting circle gathering, seen here at Notchcliff Nature Programs, which is the lab forest school for the Association for Nature-Based Education.

CREDIT: ASSOCIATION FOR NATURE-BASED EDUCATION.

Educators will incorporate a range of natural materials and artifacts, some of which can be delicate. Natural materials require special care, and some demand ongoing replenishment. If you use glass insect mounts, extra care must be taken when handling specimens, and they must be stored out of children's reach when not in use. Other natural

Here a child participates in a circle gathering with log stumps.

materials such as deer antlers are sturdy enough for children to handle on their own. There may be existing policies at your school that give guidance on handling feathers, shed snakeskin, turtle shells, and animal skulls, for example, but if not, you may need to develop them in tandem with other relevant licensing regulations. At minimum, children can observe these items and use magnification to learn more about their structure and traits. Most of the time, children can touch and explore these items, provided they wash their hands immediately afterwards. Animal bones and skulls, for example, should be thoroughly cleaned with a bleach solution before offering them to children to touch.

The best natural materials to incorporate in daily nature play invitations come from the plentiful gifts of nature in your immediate surroundings. Tree leaves and evergreen boughs, branches and sticks, dried grasses or flower heads, palm fronds, pine needles, peeling bark, seed pods, and fallen flower petals are all wonderful additions to a classroom setup, indoors or outside. (There is more description and explanation about loose parts play in Chapter 3.) By utilizing the abundant natural materials around you, children will grow more familiar and comfortable with the trees and plant life where they live, developing meaningful place-based connections to nature. It is important to remember that when you offer natural materials like these, children will explore them in many interesting ways, which includes deconstructing materials to learn about them. Consider how you display and introduce various natural materials so that children understand which ones are irreplaceable and delicate, and which ones can be thoroughly examined (and taken apart) as part of the inquiry process. It can be helpful to create a "please touch" sign to welcome exploration of natural materials and set aside another area with materials that require "gentle hands." By creating a designated place for children to examine fragile materials, this helps set an expectation of which materials can be wholly explored and which need greater care. Fabric placemats, trays, bandanas, or plexiglass mirrors can provide a visual cue and designated space to explore artifacts independently. Make a plan with staff, and involve children and families as you replenish various natural materials year-round.

Safety Measures

Nature-based learning inherently requires some specific considerations regarding policies to keep kids safe. "Safe" is a relative term, to be sure, so each program must have clear policies and procedures around the physical safety of children. Without clear and consistently applied safety policies, there are bound to be gray areas from one educator to the next, which can create not only confusion and frustration among staff but also an unsafe learning environment. In your role as a safety monitor, you are responsible for introducing, reinforcing, and intervening as needed to implement various policies. Some common considerations include tree climbing; chasing and hiding games; climbing on rocks, roots, or logs; playing with sticks; exploring near water; rough-and-tumble play; use of pretend weapons; collecting rocks, feathers, and other items; tool use; gathering around fire; holding/touching live (and dead!) animals; foraging and eating plants/fungus; and picking plants/flowers.

One of the best ways for educators to ensure children's safety is to be familiar with what's in the outdoor learning environment. It is important not only to identify but also to debunk fears about possible toxic, poisonous, and venomous plants and animals on the grounds before exploring with children. To do this, get your team of educators together to take a walk around the schoolyard and any adjacent parks or green spaces you may visit with students. Note that you'll want to do this in every season as plants change and grow over time. Begin compiling a site-specific running list of common plants and animals on your site. (Contact an area master naturalist to help, if needed.) Is there a prominent tree or row of shrubs? Are there grasses or flowering plants growing along an edge? Identify them! Take time to learn about the leaves, seeds, fruits, flowers, and in some cases the bark and branching of the most common plants and trees you will encounter. Learning about the plants and animals on the grounds will soon become a beloved aspect of the curriculum if it's not already! Take photos to document discoveries, and do research in field guides or online to learn more. As students spend more and more time outdoors, it is wonderful to involve them in the process of getting to know who lives there. Educators and students alike may be amazed to discover just how many common plants and so-called weeds have edible and medicinal uses and are important food sources for local wildlife. By learning about potentially hazardous plants and animals, educators will increase their knowledge about similar (harmless) species in the area and discover highly engaging nature-based learning opportunities. Head to your state's department of natural resources for accurate, thorough information that is relevant to your state. This may allay many of those fears about possible hazards such as poison ivy or venomous snakes in the area.

Risk Benefit Assessments (RBAs) are an important tool used to assess common risky play behaviors that may take place in nature-based programs. These assessments consider the benefits of risky activities, describe the level of risk, and outline interventions needed to engage in the activity if it is found to be beneficial to child development. *Site scans* are used daily by educators to assess, document, and avoid potential hazards in the physical learning environment. Teachers should perform a site scan before going outdoors with children to check the area for potential hazards and address them as needed before children visit the space. A daily site scan is recommended no matter what the outdoor space is and can be completed with a physical paper record or digital format. Both forms of assessment are ongoing and mandatory to ensure the well-being of staff and children alike.

RBAs and site scans can also be important tools to share with parents because they demonstrate the thoughtful care and attention given to risk management in your program. Furthermore, if an incident or injury occurs, these tools provide documentation of your daily commitment to safety in the outdoor learning environment.

> **NOTE:** *These tools enhance risk management and safety for nature-based programs. They do not replace your waivers or releases, emergency plans, or other more comprehensive policies and protocols—for example, for fire making and tool use.*

Teachers also need practical class management tips that can keep children safe. Routine use of boundary markers, auditory cues for gathering, and embedded safety routines are a few essential practices that help teachers manage groups outside the classroom. Teachers should also give special consideration for children with functional health care needs to ensure that individualized plans will support every learner.

Gearing Up to Go Outside

Each state has different guidance around weather safety, but there are commonsense guidelines to follow when deciding if weather is too hazardous to hold class outdoors. Is it 40 degrees Fahrenheit with light rainfall? Not a problem! With appropriate layered gear, including a base layer, waterproof outerwear, wool socks, and rain boots, you are good to go! It isn't the weather

Educators take time to learn common plants and animals on the school grounds, such as poison ivy and Virginia creeper, pictured here. These two plants often grow together, but on closer study, they are easily distinguished. Poison ivy has three leaves, each with slight lobes (circled). Virginia creeper has five leaves. Both are excellent food sources for wildlife.

CREDIT: MONICA WIEDEL-LUBINSKI.

Children dress comfortably in rainsuits and boots not only when it is raining but also when the ground is wet and muddy.

CREDIT: BLUESTONE VILLAGE AND NATURE PROGRAMS, SHOHOLA, PENNSYLVANIA.

that typically prevents people from going outside. Often it is a combination of (1) preparedness (or lack of preparation) to be outdoors for the current weather conditions to ensure comfort and safety and (2) training and attitudes of the adults involved. (See Julia Torquati's research discussed in Chapter 4 about perceptions of nature-based educators.)

Anyone can engage in outdoor learning in every season when they are outfitted with appropriate gear. Children can also play much more independently (and comfortably) when they are dressed for the weather and can freely move about. Programs will need to decide which gear to provide and what parents are expected to provide. Be sure to include a thorough gear list upon registration. Every program should have a gear bank with spare clothes, boots, wool socks, and waterproof mittens, among other things, to be sure every child can be prepared to go outdoors. Consider creating a private way for families to ask for help procuring gear before the school year begins. Tables 5.1 and 5.2 list examples of what children and teachers may need, depending on site-specific conditions.

Table 5.1 Children's Gear List

Summer	Fall & Spring	Winter
Light-colored tank tops or T-shirts	Layered T-shirt and/or long-sleeved shirt	Waterproof, insulated mittens
Lightweight pants (pants are better for tick protection)	Long pants	Spare pair of knit gloves to wear underneath waterproof mittens
Closed-toed sandals or sturdy hiking shoes with socks pulled over pant legs to protect from ticks	Socks that can be pulled over pant legs to protect from ticks	Thick wool socks
Rain boots	Rain pants, bibs and jacket, or rainsuit	Insulated snow boots
Rain pants and rain jacket or rainsuit	Hat (insect/sun protection)	Base layer: wool, silk, or poly long underwear, top and bottom
Swimsuit (under T-shirt and shorts or pants—optional)	Rain boots	Middle layer: long-sleeve wool or fleece sweater; for extra cold days, wear fleece pants and wool mitten mid-layers, too
Hat (insect/sun protection)	Sturdy hiking shoes or boots	Outer layer: waterproof coat with hood, insulated waterproof snow pants, wool socks, and insulated waterproof mittens
Insect repellent*	Fleece pullover or warm sweater	Warm hat such as a fitted balaclava or wool hat
Sunscreen*	Insect repellent*	Neck warmer (no scarves)
	Sunscreen*	

*Note: Be sure to obtain special permission to apply these as required for state licensing.

*Backpack should be appropriately sized for your child to carry independently.

Table 5.2 Teacher's Gear List

Year-Round	Warm Season	Cold Season
Water-resistant (or waterproof) backpack with plenty of pockets; side pockets are nice for a canteen*	Closed-toed hiking sandals	Waterproof, insulated snow boots
Closed-toed hiking shoes or boots	Insect repellent with Deet or Permethrin (spray on clothes, shoes, and backpack, not on your skin)	Thick wool socks
Rain boots	Deet-free repellent for skin	Waterproof insulated mittens (better than gloves to trap heat)
Insect repellent with Deet or Permethrin (spray on clothes, shoes, and backpack, not on your skin)	Lightweight long pants	Spare pair of waterproof insulated mittens
Deet-free repellent for skin	Lightweight socks to tuck pants into	Thin pair of knit gloves to wear inside of waterproof mittens and reusable hand/toe warmers
Comfortable long pants with pockets, such as cargo pants, hiking pants, or corduroys	Sunscreen, at least 30 SPF	Fleece-lined hat, wool is best
Layers of T-shirts and sweaters as needed; avoid cotton in wet/cold weather	Rain paints	Silk, wool, or synthetic base layers
Lightweight jacket	Lightweight rain jacket with hood	Fleece pullover and/or vest for layering
Fleece pullover or vest	Cap or hat to prevent ticks	Wool sweater for layering
Spare pair of socks (lightweight or wool, depending on season)	Hair ties	Waterproof snow pants to layer over clothes
	Cooling neck gaiter	Rain pants to wear over snow pants
		Fleece balaclava, scarf, or neck warmer
		Heavy insulated waterproof coat

Establishing a Gear Bank

By reaching out to local clothing suppliers, writing grants, or allocating dollars from the school or PTA's budget, teachers can establish a gear bank for children. This provides a constant supply of boots, coats for winter and spring/fall, waterproof mittens, hats, wool socks, rainsuits, and other items that every child can use for outdoor learning. (Also, parents may donate gear that children have outgrown.) A well-stocked gear bank eliminates the barrier of inappropriate clothing for wet or cold conditions and ensures children (and staff) are prepared. Gear banks require coordination of laundering, storage space, and monitoring of damaged or lost gear, but it is well worth the effort.

Unsafe Weather Conditions

Heavy winter coats, snow pants, wool hats and socks, and waterproof, fleece-lined mittens can help prepare children (and educators!) to spend time outside. But there are weather conditions that are too dangerous for outdoor learning, no matter what you wear or how you prepare.

Arguably the most dangerous condition for outdoor learning is when there are high winds. Even on an otherwise mild, sunny day, high winds can knock down large branches and topple trees, especially following days of heavy rain or melting snow when the ground is saturated. If there are wind advisories in your area, children should not be in forested areas. In immersive forest school settings, programs typically consider winds of 20–25 miles per hour hazardous conditions, but be sure to follow wind and weather advisories from your local authorities.

Likewise, if there are extreme heat or cold weather advisories in your area, take recommended precautions to ensure the safety of your group. Washington state, the first to pass licensing standards for immersive outdoor nature-based programs, has weather-related regulations that state the following:

Conditions that pose a health or safety risk may include, but are not limited to:

(a) Heat in excess of 100 degrees Fahrenheit or pursuant to advice of the local authority

(b) Cold less than 20 degrees Fahrenheit, or pursuant to advice of the local authority

(Foundational Quality Standards for Outdoor Nature-Based Child Care 2025)

This means that under these conditions, educators must take action. Because educators receive specific professional development to assess and address hazards in outdoor settings, they are equipped to consider the full set of circumstances that may warrant a later start time, earlier pickup, relocation to an indoor space, or cancellation of their immersive outdoor programs.

Programs should never operate outdoors if there is thunder or lightning present, or other storms or severe weather conditions in the immediate vicinity. Air-quality alerts are also important to be aware of, especially if a wildfire is nearby. Nature-based programs can utilize weather apps based on the National Oceanic and Atmospheric Administration (NOAA) for real-time weather tracking. The Environmental Protection Agency's website (https://www.airnow.gov) offers the current air quality index in your area.

NOTE: *At the time of publishing, it is unclear if this information will continue to be provided to the public through NOAA and the EPA or to what extent it will be updated. Be sure to have applicable local and state-specific guidance available at all times for the most accurate, current information.*

Waldorf-inspired programs incorporate woven baskets, wood furniture, and plants to create a calm, natural learning indoor environment. Soft colors and natural fabrics such as silk and wool add to the cozy, peaceful vibe. Gooseberry Nature School, Covington, Kentucky.

CREDIT: GOOSEBERRY NATURE SCHOOL, COVINGTON, KENTUCKY

Child arranges flowers as part of a springtime invitation. Montessori-inspired programs include materials and activities that children can explore on their own. Montessori Luna Bilingual Micro School, Pikesville, Maryland.

CREDIT: MONTESSORI LUNA BILINGUAL MICRO SCHOOL, PIKESVILLE, MARYLAND

Nature-Based Learning—Indoors!

Is nature-based learning limited to the outdoors? No! Nature-based learning can take place indoors, too. Teachers can incorporate natural elements into open-ended play and share lessons about nature, which are central to the curriculum.

Additionally, teachers can create an atmosphere that looks and feels like an extension of nature while demonstrating sustainable, earth-friendly practices. As you consider the examples provided in Table 5.3, you can see how many benefits are accessible indoors.

Classroom Aesthetics and Sustainable Practices

Creating a nature-based classroom goes beyond natural materials at learning centers. Teachers also make choices about the overall aesthetics of the classroom to bring nature inside and instill eco-friendly habits of mind. Through thoughtful classroom design, the space can have a decidedly calm, natural feel and embrace sustainable practices.

Table 5.3 Ways to Bring Nature-Based Learning Inside

Ways to Bring Nature-Based Learning Inside	Example
Building or construction area	Small twigs, tree cookies, or other natural loose parts paired with wooden blocks for building
Science area or discovery table	Leaves or pine boughs from nearby trees combined with magnifiers or tweezers for exploration
Nature museum or collections area	Abandoned nest from bluebird box or nest that fell from a tree paired with books about nests and birds
Art experiences or craft area	Natural materials used as art medium or writing implements to make art
Music or listening center	Nature sounds play to learn about animal calls and songs
Artwork displays	Branches serve as a place to hang 3D artwork
Playhouse or kitchen areas	Local stones, seeds, branches, leaves, tree cookies, or other natural materials used in pretend play; could be set out on trays, in egg cartons, bowls, or baskets
Dress-up or costume, dramatic play areas	Dress-up animal capes, crowns, wings, tails, antennae, or feet inspire dramatic play, as do animal puppets and masks
Game area	Game boards and pieces made from cut tree cross sections or other natural loose parts
Math manipulatives center	Acorns, black walnuts, sweet gumball seed pods, or pine cones used for counting, sorting, or making patterns
Technology station	Microscope used for up-close observation of natural artifacts such as bones, feathers, seashells, grass
Wildlife viewing	Bird feeder at window for wildlife observation alongside binoculars or spotting scope
Scent station	Scent jars with fragrant herbs, flowers, essential oils, tea bags, or cooking spices
Sensorial work	Playdough or clay exploration paired with natural materials such as twigs, seeds, or pressed flowers
Cultural studies	Land maps, flags, local recipes, historical artifacts, photos, or books that feature monuments or buildings of cultural significance

Ways to Bring Nature-Based Learning Inside	Example
Practical life	Pouring practice to fill watering can with water or bird feeder with seed
Tool use	Hand-drill station with a fire log to practice tapping a tree
Caring for self	Putting on one's own coat and zipping it up or organizing rain boots after coming indoors
Cooking activities	Follow a recipe using locally harvested fruits, vegetables, or herbs
Caring for class animals	Feed, clean, and care for classroom pets
Caring for indoor plants	Water, repot, and tend to indoor plants

Furnishings and materials made from elements of wood, wrought iron, or stainless steel are often more durable than plastic and can eliminate exposure to off-gassing chemicals and additives in plastic toys. Teachers can also choose earthy, natural colors and patterns for wall colors and fabrics. The following suggestions may help you create a more natural aesthetic for your indoor learning environment.

Ideas to Create a Natural Classroom Aesthetic

> Soft, calm, earthy wall colors inspired by nature
> Wooden tables, chairs, shelves, cubbies, easels
> Wool or cotton rugs
> Storage baskets made from natural fibers
> Curtains, pillows, blankets, and tablecloths made from natural fibers such as cotton, linen, and wool, and perhaps have nature-inspired prints, if available
> Photographs, informative posters, exhibits, and other wall art includes inspiration from nature, especially from local wildlife and habitats
> Nature collection shelf, nature museum, and nature corner with rotating seasonal elements
> Natural light from windows is maximized with sheer curtain panels used when needed, and warm lighting is used where possible
> Prisms that refract light and bounce rainbows on surfaces in sunlight
> Nontoxic indoor plants in hanging planters, on sills, or on shelves at children's reach so they can help care for them
> Open windows to let in fresh air, depending on the season

- Live animals or animals that are raised and released as part of citizen science projects
- Natural materials available for drawing, painting, and mark-making
- Nature-inspired items for dramatic play such as animal masks, capes, and crowns as well as animal puppets
- Designated cubbies or hooks for every child to store their belongings, including backpacks, boots, and weather-related gear

In addition to a natural classroom aesthetic, daily classroom practices are how you "walk the walk" to embody sustainable, environmentally conscious practices. These items will help you implement eco-friendly habits in the classroom.

Ideas for an Eco-Friendly Classroom
- Reusable plates, bowls, cups, and utensils
- Cloth napkins and hand towels that can be laundered
- Reusable shopping bags, totes, and baskets
- Exterior rain barrel catchment for gray water that can be used for watering plants
- Organic, whole foods for meals and snacks
- Classroom composting or vermicomposting bins
- Recycling receptacles and collection system
- Storage space that allows you to save, reuse, and repurpose materials before discarding them

Why Parents May Choose Nature-Based Programs

Keep in mind that when families choose to enroll children in nature-based programs, they are usually looking for learning that goes beyond traditional early learning standards and expectations. The reasons families choose nature-based programs are varied but often include a desire for their children to:

- Explore nature through physically active, child-directed nature play
- Learn to identify features of the natural world (i.e., plants, animals, habitats)
- Develop genuine care and concern for nature
- Engage in developmentally appropriate actions to conserve, protect, and respect nature
- Cultivate a sense of belonging as part of the natural world
- Participate in activities that support meaningful nature connection

A natural outgrowth of these nature-based program components are values that families may also hope their child will develop, including empathy, mindfulness, compassion, and gratitude. The adventurous spirit of nature play also means parents are eager to learn how their children build confidence to take risks, become more determined and resilient, problem-solve with peers, and expand their creativity in natural settings and with natural materials. Given these unique features of nature-based programs, you can see how assessment takes on a greener hue.

Nature-Based Program Evaluation

It requires a great deal of thought and commitment to assess a child's nature connection and determine to what extent nature-based skills and values are helping to shape their overall development. Yet authentic assessment methods that include observation and documentation are an excellent way to evaluate each child's progress in a nature-based context (see the appendix in Chapter 3, "Nature Play and Emergent Curriculum: Perfect Partners").

Similarly, educators and administrators should implement strategies that evaluate programmatic approaches to the implementation of nature-based (and emergent) curriculum, risk management protocol, health and safety practices, and so on. Because the vision and educational philosophy of nature-based programs aim to support nature connection, ecological identity, and environmental literacy, additional tools that are tailored to measure attainment of these concepts are needed. By utilizing a comprehensive approach to evaluation, programs can first identify their strengths and challenges, then reflect on opportunities for growth to help reach their goals as a nature-based early childhood education program.

To this end, continuous reflection allows a steady flow of feedback to inform updates or changes a program may need to make to better serve the learning community. The following chart offers different methods of evaluation and sample questionnaires.

It must be stated that these forms of evaluation can be customized and applied to formal and informal evaluation with teachers, children, or the program as a whole. These forms are focused on programmatic evaluation and evaluation of teaching practices, activities, and experiences. (While this book touches on child assessment in nature-based learning, it cannot be thoroughly examined within the scope of this book.)

NOTE: Practitioner Guide to Assessing Connection to Nature *by Gabby Salazar, Kristen Kunkle, and Martha C. Monroe is an excellent resource for measurement tools and approaches that have been vetted through peer-reviewed research (Salazar et al. 2020).*

As with any form of evaluation, after you determine what you want to evaluate, choose a method of evaluation, and do the work to collect feedback, you aren't yet finished! The process continues by analyzing feedback and creating action steps to implement change as needed. Some programs rely on logic models, while others use an action plan or theory of change. A continuous rotation of evaluation activities include:

› Identify an area for evaluation
› Select a method of evaluation that includes measurable data points
› Gather information, data, and/or feedback
› Share feedback, then reflect and analyze data
› Create a strategic plan, action plan, or other action items needed for improvement
› Implement a plan to effect positive change
› Identify an area for evaluation (to determine effectiveness of plan implementation)

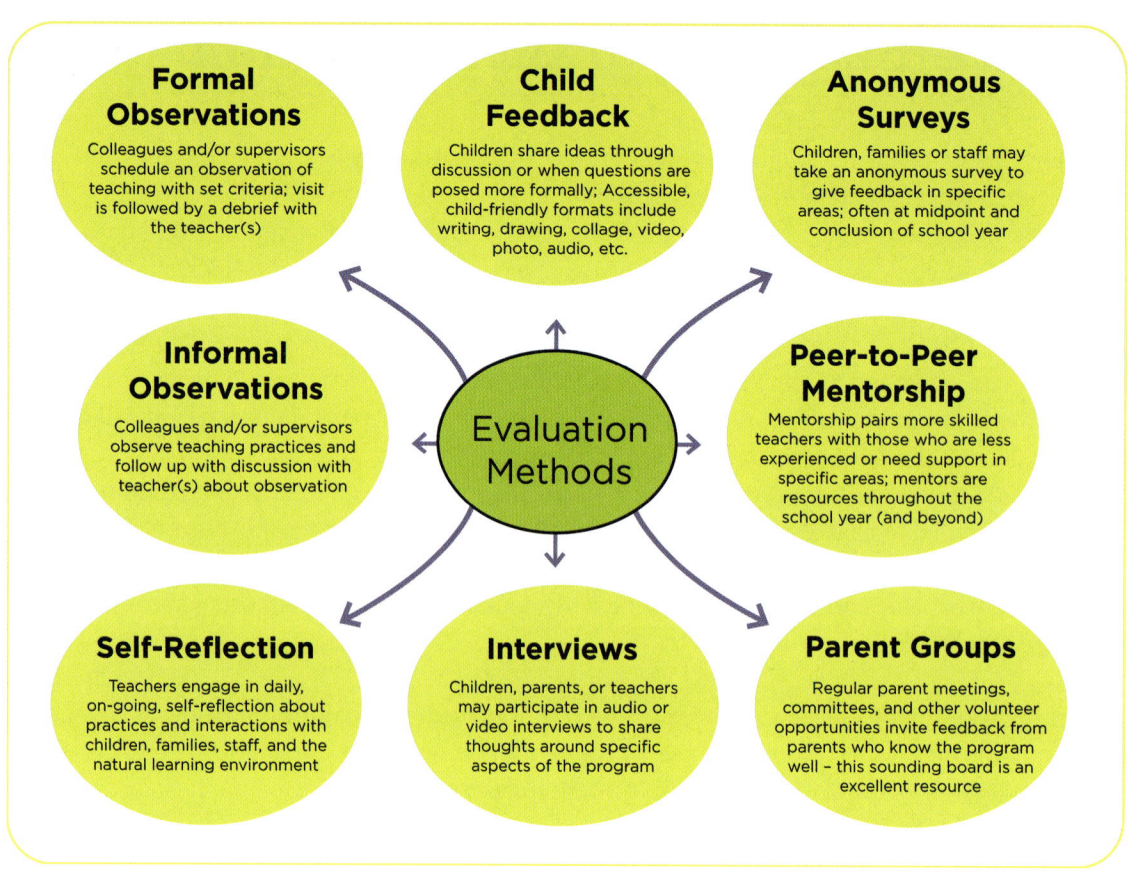

Methods of Evaluation

These activities can look vastly different depending on the vision, mission, and educational philosophy of the nature-based program. Some programs may rely on evidence-based tools or standards for evaluation, while others craft customized tools that assess specific program goals and outcomes. For example, program evaluation methods would look different for a program with a uniquely marine or aquatic emphasis that raises and releases oysters or incorporates fishing along local waterways. Another nature-based program may have an interdisciplinary nature-arts focus with a performance or gallery aspect. Some may include full language immersion, such as one in Spanish, while another may involve daily farming, animal husbandry, or equine care. While any nature-based program may participate in these activities if they are central to the program's ethos, evaluation methods should be tailored to understand how program goals are attained in context.

Nature-based programming requires that a different approach is applied to the basic principles of managing a high-quality early childhood program. The learning environment, safety protocols, assessment strategies, and family partnerships must be viewed through the lens of the natural world and reflect the opportunities for unique learning experiences and all the benefits that nature provides. Not only can you implement nature-based offerings in your community, but you can also assess their effectiveness to reveal the positive impacts you have as a nature-based program.

Unearthing Joy: Transforming Outdoor Spaces into Cultural Places

By Ashley Brailsford, PhD, Founding Director, Unearthing Joy, Nashville, Tennesee

What does a nature education program look like that marries the philosophy of multicultural education with nature-based education? What can a program look like that centers the roles and narratives of Indigenous, Black, and other People of the Global Majority in nature education?

I started to explore answers to these questions after looking into nature education programs for my own son, who is Black and had just turned 6 years old in the summer of 2020. I knew I was not ready to send him back to school amongst the uncertainty of COVID-19, but I felt he would be safe outdoors around other children. And I knew it was important for both of us to have community as we embarked on homeschooling. When I looked into nature education, not surprisingly, all the programs were in predominantly White areas. I did not feel comfortable sending him into programs full-time where he would be the only Black child, so I started the journey of creating my own program, Unearthing Joy, by answering many of the questions that are outlined in this chapter.

Our first program was a one-and-a-half hour visit to a poultry farmer friend, Ms. Cynthia. I was amazed to see a Black woman caring for over 300 birds. Even more fascinating was her story of being a trauma nurse from Chicago that did not have any experience on farms growing up but knew in her heart she always loved birds. When she moved to Nashville, she embarked on learning about poultry and today teaches about the importance of conserving various breeds while also running her farm. She was a gracious host and prepared a scavenger hunt activity for the children where they had to find the birds matching the pictures of various breeds. After watching Ms. Cynthia share her journey, I read the book *Preaching to the Chickens* by Jabari Asim, which is about how civil rights leader John Lewis became a confident speaker … by preaching to chickens on his farm as a child. Learning about Ms. Cynthia's journey, reading Asim's book, and the children and adults participating in the scavenger hunt activity became the basis for Unearthing Joy's immersive programming format for young children.

Over the next season our programming evolved from a once-a-month offering to a six-to-eight-week spring and fall series at a community garden that is in a historically Black neighborhood in Nashville and owned by a Black woman, Ms. Pearl. This is also significant to how Unearthing Joy does its programming because our spaces and lands along with the people (living and ancestors) who inhabit them serve as curriculum. We are intentional about inviting culturally diverse people to share their gifts and talents with our families. We are intentional about the books and stories that we share. And we are intentional about stating that we center Indigenous, Black, and other People of the Global Majority. We have created series based on community interests and those of the children that include "Gardening for Food Justice," "Exploring the Animal Kingdom," and "Creative Arts in Nature and Skills for Liberation." We hope to inspire other programs to use their community and lands as curriculum and unearth important cultural stories and joy.

CALL TO ACTION

> Begin a daily Sit Spot practice. Select an outdoor location that you can visit daily for at least 10 consecutive days for 20 minutes per visit. Remember, the purpose is to sit still in observation with your senses, no matter the weather. No cell phones, journals, or other distractions—just mindful stillness in nature.

NOTE: *Sit Spots are wonderful for toddlers and preschoolers, too! The time frame will be much shorter, but children also love this core routine.* The Other Way to Listen *by Byrd Baylor and illustrated by Peter Parnall is a wonderful literacy tie-in.*

> Outline three short-term steps you can take to positively impact the amount of time children are engaged in unstructured nature play experiences that afford risky play. Include accommodations that may be needed.

> Describe three ways your nature-based program honors children.

Reflection Questions

> When planning a nature-based program, what steps can you take to honor the backgrounds and identities of all children within the learning community?

> What barriers to outdoor learning exist for children with disabilities in your program? What can you do to mitigate them?

> How will you encourage a deeper nature connection for children, families, and staff?

> What are some methods of evaluation you would like to incorporate into your program?

Appendix: Getting to Know You

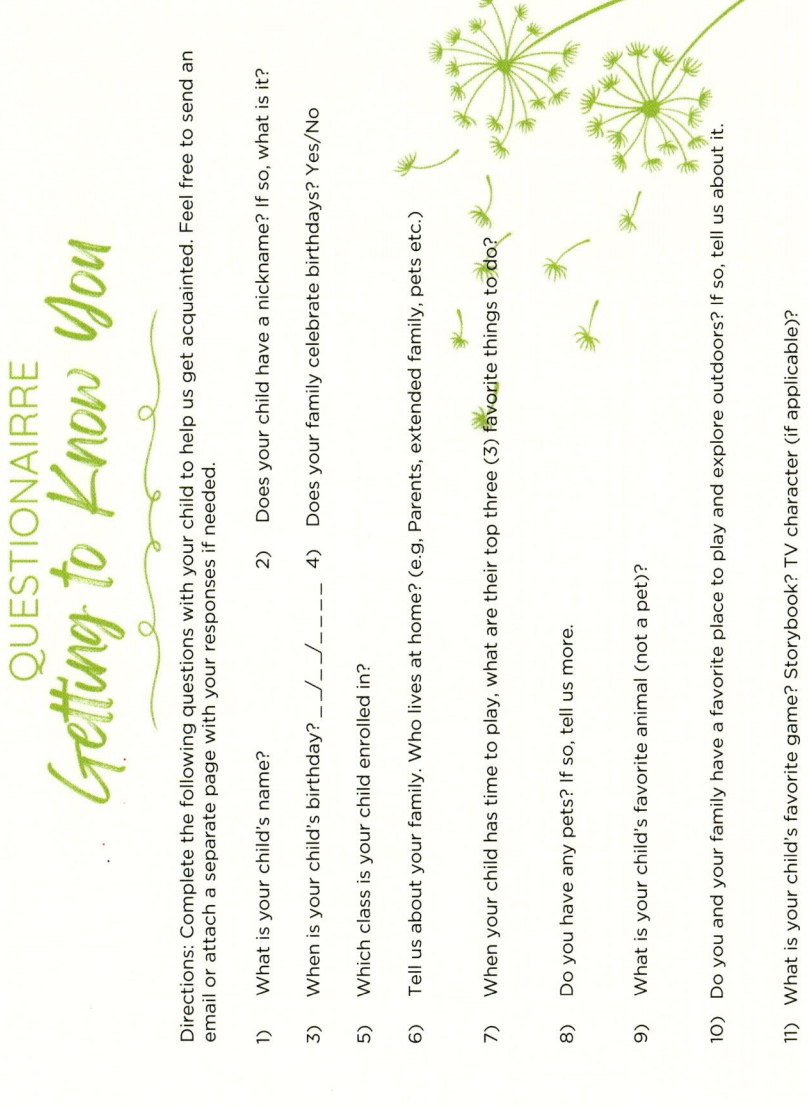

QUESTIONAIRRE
Getting to Know You

Directions: Complete the following questions with your child to help us get acquainted. Feel free to send an email or attach a separate page with your responses if needed.

1) What is your child's name?

2) Does your child have a nickname? If so, what is it?

3) When is your child's birthday? _ _/_ _/_ _ _ _

4) Does your family celebrate birthdays? Yes/No

5) Which class is your child enrolled in?

6) Tell us about your family. Who lives at home? (e.g. Parents, extended family, pets etc.)

7) When your child has time to play, what are their top three (3) favorite things to do?

8) Do you have any pets? If so, tell us more.

9) What is your child's favorite animal (not a pet)?

10) Do you and your family have a favorite place to play and explore outdoors? If so, tell us about it.

11) What is your child's favorite game? Storybook? TV character (if applicable)?

Questionnaires

QUESTIONAIRRE
Getting to Know You

12) What do you consider your child's greatest gifts and strengths to be?

13) Explain areas of challenging behavior or skills that your child/family is actively working on.

14) Describe any physical, social, emotional, intellectual, or behavioral challenges we should be aware of.

15) Tell us about any other health conditions, learning differences, or preferences that will help us support your child.

16) What is your primary goal for your child in this program?
    o To play and explore nature
    o To make friends and socialize in a relaxed, natural learning environment
    o To hone academic skills (reading, writing, math, science, etc.)
    o To develop a greater sense of nature connection
    o To minimize risk of potential illness through outdoor learning
    o To provide an active outlet for movement and physical skill development
    o To child childcare for when I am at work
    o Other:

17) Describe what your hopes and intentions are for your child in our program this year. What do you hope your child will gain from the experience?

18) Upload or bring in one photo of your child and one photo of your family here.

Please include any other thoughts you have to share below. Thank you for completing the survey.

Questionnaires (continued)

Nature-Based Early Childhood Education

Index

Note: Page numbers followed by *f* and *t* indicate figures and tables, respectively.

A

administrators, supporting educators, 99–104, 107
aesthetic, biophilic value with description, 18
All Work and No Play (Almon), 55
Almon, Joan, 55
American Academy of Pediatrics, 22
American Nature Study Society (ANSS), 3
Americans with Disabilities Act (ADA), 117
animal forms, nature connection, 98
animals, encounters in nature, 43–44
anonymous surveys, evaluation method, 134
Anthony, Carl, 5
Antioch University, 102
artifacts, 80
Asim, Jabari, 135
Association for Nature-Based Education (ANBE), xii, 7, 77, 102, 104
atelier, Reggio Emilia approach, 85
attention deficit hyperactivity disorder (ADHD)
  definition, 36
  reduced effects of, 36–37
attention/impulse control, 35
Attention Restoration Theory (ART), 34
Auchlone Nature Kindergarten, 80
Audubon Naturalist Society, xii
Aventuras Forest School, bilingual learning, 14–16
Ayers, Jean, 25
Ayers Sensory Integration (ASI), 25

B

Bailie, Patti, 9
Balanced and Barefoot (Hanscom), 24, 74
Baltimore City Recreation and Parks, xiii
Bashwanji, Yash, 9
Beam, Amy, 104
Biedrzycki, Julie, 102
Biermeier, Mary Ann, 78
Bilingual Learning at Forest School, Gonzalez, 14–16
biophilia, concept of, 33
biophilia hypothesis, 17
  values with descriptions, 17–18
Black Faces, White Spaces (Finney), 113–114
Black narratives, 135
Blackwell, Sarah, 30
Bluestone Village and Nature Programs, children making fairy village, 1
Braiding Sweetgrass (Kimmerer), 71
Brailsford, Ashley, 135

C

Carr, Margaret, 80
Carrie Murray Nature Center, xii
Carson, Rachel, 3
chalk, 38
changeable books, 80
Chawla, Louise, 9
child-directed learning
  comparing teacher-directed and, 59
  term, 29
child feedback, evaluation method, 134
children
  cognitive and intellectual development, 34–37
  joy in the forest, 77
  language development, 38–47
  nature-based programs, 112–119
  outdoor gear list, 126
  physical development, 22–28
  social and emotional development, 28–34
  strategies for outdoor learning challenges, 114–116
  unstructured play for, with disabilities, 67–69
  with disabilities, 117–119
Children & Nature Network, 102
children's books and poetry, 45–46
circle gathering, rhythm of the day, 62
Civilian Conservation Corps (CCC), 3
classroom aesthetics, nature-based indoor learning, 129–132
Clean Air Act (1970), 4
Clean Water Act (1972), 4
closing circle, rhythm of the day, 63
co-creating a curriculum, concept of, 78
cognitive and intellectual development, 34–37
  blossoming imagination, 36
  executive functioning skills, 35–36
  greater engagement, 37
  reduced affects of ADHD, 36–37

cognitive and intellectual development (*continued*)
   skills and values, 50–51
collaboration, nature-based educators, 100–101
collage, nature journals, 40
compassion, 31–32
Comstock, Anna Botsford, 3
consent, 31
cooking, 46
Coolidge, Calvin, 3
cooperation, 31
Cornell, Joseph, 86
Cornell Lab, 39
Cornell University, 3
COVID-19 pandemic, 16, 135
Coyote's Guide to Connecting with Nature, The (Young, Haas, and McGown), 86, 98
creative arts, flow learning, 86
creativity, autonomy, and play (CAP), 36
cultivating values, 31–32
cycle of planning, emergent curriculum, 82–84

D

daily rhythm
   emergent curriculum, 85–86
   50/50 principle, 64
   learning, 61–64
   sample, 62–63
dandelion fritter recipe, 47
developmental domains, skills and values, 49–52
dictating, nature journals, 41
disabilities
   program for children with, 117–119
   unstructured play for children with, 67–69
documentation
   emergent curriculum, 79–81
   methods for, 79–80
   nature journals, 41
documentation panels, 80
Dodge Nature Center, xii
dominionistic, biophilic value with description, 18
dramatic play, 42
drawing and mark-making, nature journals, 39–40

E

early childhood learning, affordances of nature for, 6–8
Earth Day, 4
Eastern Region Association of Forest and Nature Schools, xii, 13
ecologistic-scientific, biophilic value with description, 18
ecophobia, 91
emergent curriculum
   cycle of planning, 82–84
   daily rhythm, 85–86
   definition, 78
   nature play and, 78–88
   observation and documentation, 79–81
   understanding through nature play, 81–86
Emile, or a Treatise on Education (Rousseau), 6
emotional well-being, 33–34
empathy, 31
environmental education
   definition, 5
   growth of, 5–6
   roots of, 3–5
   term, 6
environmental literacy, 5, 34
   skills and values, 51–52
Environmental Protection Agency, 128
E.O. Wilson Foundation, 17
equitable nature-based learning, challenges to, 13–16
Ernst, Julie, 9
executive functioning skills, 35–36
experience, nature-based educators, 95–96
experiential learning, 13, 16, 57

F

families
   choosing nature-based programs, 132
   cultivating trust and respect with, 119–121

field guides
   children's, 45–46
   nature connection, 98
50/50 principle, daily rhythm, 64
Finch, Ken, 9
Finney, Carolyn, 113
Floorbooks, 80
flow learning, 86
Ford, Phyllis, 6
forest, term, 11
forest bathing workshop, 103
forest days, 11
Forest Days Handbook, A (Minnucci and Teachout), 11
Forest Days Outdoor Learning Program, 48, 74, 77
forest kindergarten, 10–11
Forest Learning Collective, 86
forest preschool, 10–11
Forest School Association, 11
Forest Schools Education, 30
forgiveness, 31
formal observations, evaluation method, 134
friendship, 31

G

Gallagher, Hannah, 67–69
games, 44
Getting to Know You, questionnaire, 137–138
Gill, Tim, 9
Gonzalez, Pilar, 14–16
Gooseberry Nature School, 129
gratitude, 32
Great Depression, 3

H

Haas, Ellen, 86
Handbook for Nature Study, The (Comstock), 3
Hanscom, Angela, 24, 74
hazard, definition, 73
hear, developing, 23
homeschooling, 135
honorable harvest, 71
hot executive control (HEC), 35

humanistic, biophilic value with description, 18
human-nature connection, 2

I

imagination, blossoming, 36
iNaturalist, 39
independence, 30
    outdoor settings, 72–74, 76
Indigenous people
    land acknowledgements, 4
    roles and narratives of, 135
Individuals with Disabilities Education Act (IDEA), 117
indoor learning, nature-based, 129–132
informal observations, evaluation method, 134
inquiry process, 43
interoception sense, developing, 25
interviews, evaluation method, 134
invitation, term, 62
invitations
    daily rhythm sample, 62
    nature play samples, 89
Irvine Nature Center, xi, xii, 107

J

Jackman, Wilbur, 3
journaling, nature connection, 99
joy in the forest, 77

K

Kenny, Erin, 9
Kimmerer, Robin Wall, 71
Knight, Sara, 9
Kunkle, Kristen, 133

L

labeling, nature journals, 41
language development, 38–47
    children's books and poetry, 45–46
    cooking, 46
    dramatic play, 42
    encounters with animals and other surprises in nature, 43–44
    field guides, 39
    games, 44
    local history, 47
    maps, 39
    music and song, 41–42
    names and signs, 41
    nature journals, 39–41
    questioning, 43
    skills and values, 51
    storytelling, 38
Larimore, Rachel, 9
Last Child in the Woods (Louv), 10
learning schedule, daily rhythm, 61–64
Learning Stories approach, 80
Lee, Wendy, 80
Lewis, John, 135
LGBTQ+ community, 121
Lime Hollow Nature Center, 103
listening for bird language, nature connection, 99
literacy development, skills and values, 51
local history, 47
loose parts play
    materials for, 70
    natural materials, 69, 70
    using and respecting natural materials, 71–72
Louv, Richard, 10

M

McGee, Margaret Embers, 41
McGown, Evan, 86
Malaguzzi, Loris, 13, 85
Mapmaking with Children (Sobel), 39
mapping, nature connection, 98
maps, 39
Mata-McMahon, Jennifer, 32
Mayo Clinic, 22
mentorship, 100–101
    evaluation method, 134
Migratory Bird Treaty Act, 71
Miller, Maryfaith Decker, 86
mindfulness, 32–33
mind's-eye imagining, nature connection, 99
Minnucci, Eliza, 11
Monroe, Martha C., 133
Montessori, Maria, 12
Montessori Luna Bilingual Micro School, 129
Montessori Method, teaching, 12
moralistic, biophilic value with description, 18
mud kitchen, 46, 122
multicultural education, nature-based, 135
music and song, 41–42

N

names and signs, 41
National Association for the Education of Young Children, 114
National Conference on Outdoor Recreation, 3
National Oceanic and Atmospheric Administration (NOAA), 128
naturalistic, biophilic value with description, 17
Naturally Inclusive (Wilson), 117
natural materials
    loose parts play, 70
    using and respecting, 71–72
Natural Start Alliance, 13, 102
nature
    commitment to, 100
    connecting with, 17
    teachers of, 94
    term, 2
nature-based classroom, atelier, 85
nature-based curriculum, program's vision, 100
nature-based early childhood education (NBECE), xi, xii, xiv–xv
    benefits of, 52–53
    concept of, 2
    description of, 8–13
    examples of programs, 10–11
    kindred spirits to, 12–13
    principles of, xiii–xiv

nature-based education
　blazing a trail in, xi–xiii
　Reggio Emilia approach and, 86–88
nature-based educators
　administrators supporting, 99–104, 107
　changing perceptions, 94
　collaboration as team, 100–101
　committing to nature, 100
　connecting with nature, 96–99
　creating strong roots, 93
　experience and qualifications, 95–96
　ongoing professional development, 101–103
　orientation and preparation, 100
　reflective teaching practices, 103–104
　self-reflection for teachers, 104–105
　teacher self-care, 103
nature-based indoor learning, 129–132
　ideas for eco-friendly classroom, 132
　ideas for natural classroom aesthetic, 131–132
　parents choosing, 132
　ways to bring inside, 130–131
nature-based learning, 57
　benefits of, 48–52
　challenges to equitable, 13–16
　greater engagement, 37
nature-based learning and play
　emergent curriculum, 81–86
　lived experience of, 66
　playful behaviors, 64–66
nature-based program(s)
　administration, 110
　bringing learning indoors, 129–132
　children's gear list, 126
　children with disabilities, 117–118
　commitment to every child, 112–119
　cultivating trust and respect with families, 119–121
　evaluation, 133–134
　foundational program components, 110
　gear bank, 127
　gearing up to go outside, 125–128
　methods of evaluation, 134
　planning for the day-to-day, 121–128
　safety measures, 123–125
　strategies for challenges in outdoor learning, 114–116
　teacher's gear list, 127
　teaching and learning approaches, 111
　trail map for planning, 109–111
　unsafe weather conditions, 128
Nature-Based Teacher Certification, 101, 102, 103
nature connection, 1, 17, 34
　core routines, 98–99
　teaching, 96–99
　ways for teachers to nurture, 97
nature days, 11
nature educators, 94
nature journals, 39–41, 53
nature kindergarten, 10
nature museum, 82
nature pedagogy, 8
nature play, 28
　emergent curriculum, 78–88
　invitations, 89
　joy in the forest, 77
　loose parts play, 69, 70
　playful behaviors, 64–66
　simplicity of, 58, 60
　teacher-guided vs. teacher-directed, 56, 58
　understanding emergent curriculum, 81–86
　understanding skills, content and values, 48–52
nature preschool, 10
nature school, 11
nature study, beginnings of, 2–3
Nature Study for the Common School (Jackman), 3

nature surprises, encounters, 43–44
negativistic, biophilic value with description, 18
Neufert, Hermann, 3
Nicholson, Simon, 69
Nixon, Richard, 4
North American Association of Environmental Education (NAAEE), 5
Northern Illinois Nature Preschool Association, 13
nutrition, child development, 26–28

O

observation, emergent curriculum, 79–81
Outdoor Education (Ford), 6
outdoor learning
　attitudes and understanding, 91–92
　benefits for kids needing, 7
　children's gear list, 126
　days, 11
　establishing a gear bank, 127
　gearing up for, 125–128
　strategies and considerations for, 114–116
　teacher's gear list, 127
　unsafe weather conditions, 128
outdoor recreation, term, 6
outdoor settings, risky play and independence, 72–74, 76
Outdoor Teacher Retreats, 102

P

paints and dyes, nature journals, 40
parent groups, evaluation method, 134
peer-to-peer mentorship, evaluation method, 134
Pegnataro, Justin, 47
People of the Global Majority, 135
perseverance, 28–29
photographs, nature journals, 40–41

physical development
    children, 22–28
    developing the senses, 23–25
    nourishing our bodies, 26–28
    skills and values, 49
Place-Based Education (Sobel), 27
place-based education (PBE), 27
planning cycle, emergent curriculum, 82–84
play, education, 55
play-based learning, 55–58, *see also* nature play
poetry, children's books and, 45
Preaching to the Chickens (Asim), 135
Prescott College, 102
pretend play, 42
printmaking, nature journals, 40
professional development, nature-based educators, 101–103
proprioceptive sense, developing, 24
provocation, term, 62

Q

qualifications, nature-based educators, 95–96
questioning, 43
    nature connection, 98
questionnaire, Getting to Know You, 137–138
Quiet Crisis, The (Sears), 3

R

Race, Poverty, and the Environment (Anthony), 5
reflective teaching, nature-based educators, 103–104
Reggio Emilia Approach
    atelier, 85
    invitation, 62
    learning, 13
    nature-based education and, 86–88
resilience, 29–30

risk benefit assessments (RBAs), 124
risky play, 72–76
Rivkin, Mary, 9
Roosevelt, Franklin, 3
Rousseau, Jean-Jacques, 6
rubbings, nature journals, 40
rule of 100, 71
rules, games, 44

S

safe, term, 123
safety measures, nature-based learning, 123–125
Salazar, Gabby, 133
"Salt Songs," 42
Sandseter, Ellen, 9, 72
Schein, Deborah, 33
Seattle Children's PlayGarden, 67, 68, 69, 118
self-care, teacher, 103
self-confidence, 30
self-reflection
    evaluation method, 134
    teachers, 104–105
Sense of Wonder, The (Carson), 4
senses
    developing the, 23–25
    nature connection, 98
Serviceberry, The (Kimmerer), 71
sewing, nature journals, 40
shared vision, nature-based curriculum, 100, 101
Sharing Nature with Children (Cornell), 86
sight, developing, 23
Silent Spring (Carson), 3
Simmons, Bora, 9
sit spot, nature connection, 98, 136
smashing, nature journals, 40
smell, developing, 23
smooshing, nature journals, 40
Sobel, David, 9, 27, 39
social and emotional development
    cultivating values, 31–32
    emotional well-being and stress relief, 33–34

friendship and cooperation, 31
mindfulness and spirituality, 32–33
nature connection and environmental literacy, 34
perseverance, 28–29
resilience, 29–30
self-confidence and independence, 30
skills and values, 49
songlines, 42
spiritual development, skills and values, 51
spirituality, 32–33
STAR Institute for Sensory Processing, 25
Steiner, Rudolph, 12
stories, children's, 45–46
Storypark app, 80, 86–87
storytelling, 38
    nature connection, 98
stress relief, 33–34
surprises in nature, 43–44
survival living, nature connection, 99
sustainable practices, nature-based indoor learning, 129–132
symbolic, biophilic value with description, 18

T

taste, developing, 23
teacher(s)
    nurturing nature connection, 97
    outdoor gear list, 127
    sample rhythm of the day, 62–63
    self-reflection, 104–105
teacher-directed learning, 56, 58
    comparing child-directed and, 59
teacher-guided learning, 56, 58
Teachout, Meghan, 11
team collaboration, 100–101
thanksgiving, nature connection, 99
"Theory of Loose Parts" (Nicholson), 69

topophilia, term, 17
Torquati, Julia, 9, 94
touch, developing, 23–24
Tovey, Helen, 76
tracing, nature journals, 40
tracking, nature connection, 98
trail map, planning a nature-based program, 109–111
Tuan, Yi-Fu, 17
tuberculosis, 3

U

"Unearthing Joy" (Brailsford), 135
University of Maryland, Baltimore County (UMBC), 32

unstructured play, children with disabilities, 67–69
utilitarian, biophilic value with description, 17

V

vestibular sense, developing, 24–25
vitamin D, 26, 27
Vygotsky, Lev, 35

W

Waldorf education, 12–13
wandering, nature connection, 98
Warden, Claire, 9, 80
Washington Nature Preschool Association, 13

Watson, Marty, 9
weather conditions, unsafe, 128
weaving, nature journals, 40
Williams Ridge, Sheila, 9
Wilson, E. O., 17, 33
Wilson, Ruth, 9, 117

Y

Young, Jon, 9, 86

Z

Zone of Proximal Development (ZPD), 35